'This new book brings to light the ric prayer, distinct in its theology, method provides an illuminative explanation it unfolds through the charism of Francis of Assisi, deepened by the contemplative gaze of Clare of Assisi, and drawn into an incarnational theology in Bonaventure and Jacopone da Todi. The inclusion of contemporary Franciscans at prayer reminds the reader that this vibrant path to God is active and alive today, a path that is deeply incarnational, profoundly ecological and livelily communal. I highly recommend this book to all who seek the Franciscan way to God.'
Ilia Delio OSF, Connelly Chair in Theology, Villanova University, Pennsylvania

'This Lent book is a rich and inspiring resource for all spiritual seekers who want to live the gospel more fully and follow Christ more closely – to become a living prayer. Dan Horan opens up the inclusive and diverse Franciscan tradition to reveal that there is a path for everyone; all are invited to discover and renew a closer relationship to God, others and creation through a deeper experience of different ways of praying.'
Fiona Gardner, author of *Taking Heart*

'The Franciscan spiritual tradition is long, rich, varied and not widely enough known. Dan Horan's wonderfully clear book brings us into living contact with the breadth of this tradition and the ways of prayer it opens up. A wonderful Lenten guide.'
Karen Kilby, Bede Professor of Catholic Theology, University of Durham

'St Francis of Assisi was originally called by God to rebuild, or reform, the Church. His life and ministry represented a complete revolution in the Church, a turning back to the origin: that is, to Jesus. This is why Francis is such a powerful model for Lent, which also asks us to rebuild, reform and recommit ourselves to the Christian journey. Daniel Horan OFM, a gifted writer and theologian, and a Franciscan himself, is the perfect person to lead us on this journey of renewal, with his great forebear, Francis of Assisi.'

James Martin SJ, author of *Learning to Pray* and *Jesus: A Pilgrimage*

'All of the Franciscan wisdom figures in this Lenten guide were profoundly drawn to the mystery of Christ. Classic themes in prayer and the Christian life, such as poverty, the cross, creation, Incarnation and solitude, are covered. Daniel Horan beautifully conveys the simplicity, breadth and humanity of the Franciscan approach.'

Richard Rohr OFM, Center for Action and Contemplation, Albuquerque, New Mexico

'Daniel Horan's study of Francis and prayer takes the wider view of prayer within the whole Franciscan tradition, explaining that Francis, whose theological background was limited, did not set out to teach a method or system of praying, but his spirituality was expressed in his life rather than in written form. So, along with Francis himself, this book investigates with great originality other Franciscan saints – Clare (who did teach prayer), Bonaventure (who was a mystic, as well as a theologian), Angela of Foligno (a mystic in everyday life), John Duns Scotus (another theologian), Catherine of Bologna (a highly educated woman of her day), and Solanus Casey (a modern-day Franciscan who began life working on his father's farm). The differing circumstances and temperaments of these saints and blessed ones demonstrates the diversity of the Franciscan prayer experience and shows how each of these holy ones adds his or her own distinctive elements and broadens the spiritual landscape of resources available in the way of the Franciscans: there is something for everyone in the Franciscan tradition. At the same time, Horan shows clearly that there are certain elements of similarity across these examples: the importance of the gospel; the centrality of the person of Christ and his Passion and the innate goodness of the world, of creation and of humanity. And Franciscan prayer is not just a matter of engaging the mind and the heart but

it also demands imitation: "Follow the teaching and footprints of Jesus Christ." To quote Horan: "Prayer is the lifeblood of one's faith journey, which not only anchors us in our Christian belief but also fuels and animates our living the gospel in the times and places we find ourselves." In this book, he shows us how to follow in the footsteps of the Franciscan saints – which is the following of Christ himself – to do just that. This carefully researched book, which brings these saints to life, is a precious companion to be read and reread, not just during Lent but throughout the year, and will appeal to anyone who desires to follow Christ more closely and to deepen his or her own prayer life.'
Patricia Rumsey OSC, Abbess, Poor Clare Monastery, Barnet

'Few persons have influenced Christianity as deeply as has Francis of Assisi. Francis, in effect, reshaped Christianity's romantic imagination. These reflections by Daniel Horan arise out of that romantic, Franciscan imagination. They are reflections on prayer, extrapolated from the giants within the Franciscan tradition, rich in their heterogeneity, offering something for every temperament. This is not your average book on prayer. With his exceptional ability to tailor academic thought to aching pastoral need, Daniel Horan is becoming an increasingly important voice in spirituality today.'
Ronald Rolheiser OMI, Oblate School of Theology, San Antonio, Texas

Daniel P. Horan OFM is the Duns Scotus Professor of Spirituality at Catholic Theological Union in Chicago, where he teaches systematic theology and spirituality; a columnist for the *National Catholic Reporter*, and the author of more than twelve books, including *Catholicity and Emerging Personhood: A Contemporary Theological Anthropology* (2019), *The Franciscan Heart of Thomas Merton: A New Look at the Spiritual Inspiration of His Life, Thought, and Writing* (2014), and *Dating God: Live and Love in the Way of St. Francis* (2012). He is also the co-host of *The Francis Effect Podcast*.

THE WAY OF THE FRANCISCANS

A prayer journey through Lent

Daniel P. Horan

First published in Great Britain in 2021

Society for Promoting Christian Knowledge
36 Causton Street
London SW1P 4ST
www.spck.org.uk

British Library Cataloguing-in-Publication Data
A catalogue record for this book is available from the British Library

ISBN 978–0–281–08317–6
eBook ISBN 978–0–281–08318–3

1 3 5 7 9 10 8 6 4 2

Typeset by Manila Typesetting Company
First printed in Great Britain by Ashford Colour Press

eBook by Manila Typesetting Company

Produced on paper from sustainable forests

Contents

Introduction

The diversity of Franciscan prayer

There is perhaps no better time to explore the richness of the Franciscan spiritual tradition than during Lent. Lent is known as a penitential season, a period in which Christian believers devote themselves more fully to prayer, fasting, and charitable acts during a window of time designed to commemorate the forty days that Jesus Christ spent praying and fasting in the desert (Matthew 4.1–11; Mark 1.12–13; Luke 4.1–13). It is a time of preparation for Easter marked by spiritual renewal and reflection on how one is living the Christian life, ultimately aimed at embracing the divine call to continuing conversion (*metanoia* in Greek). What makes this a fortuitous time for exploring the Franciscan way of prayer is that the whole of the Franciscan spiritual tradition is grounded in a commitment to penance modelled by Francis (c. 1182–1226) and Clare of Assisi (1194–1253). In fact, so central is the theme of penance in the spiritual life of Francis that he opened his final testament dictated shortly before his death with these words:

> The Lord gave me, Brother Francis, thus to begin doing penance in this way: for when I was in sin, it seemed too bitter for me to see lepers. And the Lord Himself led me among them and I showed mercy to them. And when I left them, what had seemed bitter to me was turned into sweetness of soul and body. And afterwards I delayed a little and left the world.[1]

As Franciscan scholars have noted, Francis's *Testament* is the most autobiographical of any of the extant texts we have from the thirteenth-century saint.[2] These opening lines reflect the

1

recollections of a man considering the extraordinary journey of his short life and the manner in which God accomplished so much through his own simple desire to live the gospel more fully and follow Christ more closely. And Francis describes the totality of this experience as one of penance. The desire to live this way occurred early in his twenties during a time of uncertainty and vocational discernment following experiences of battle and having been a prisoner of war. It began as a personal journey of conversion, but it quickly grew into more than the story of one person's pilgrimage of faith. Franciscan scholars Regis Armstrong and Ingrid Peterson explain:

> From his writings, it might be concluded that he simply wanted to live the fullness of life he received at his baptism, but in a short period of time men and women began to follow his vision of a poor and simple Trinitarian life. As does Jesus, so too his follower Francis continues to draw vast numbers of followers.[3]

Those who would follow him, including Clare of Assisi quite early on, were drawn to the vision of Christian spiritual life he exemplified. Unlike some forms of religious life common at the time, and perhaps even more common today, which are distinguished by complex *regulae* (that is, 'rules' of religious life) and programmes of asceticism and schedules of prayer, the Franciscan vision is deceptively simple: 'to observe the Holy Gospel of Our Lord Jesus Christ'.[4] That simplicity can help explain the broad appeal the early Franciscan movement had, drawing thousands and thousands of women and men, professed religious sisters and brothers as well as laypeople, to this form of Christian living. It helps account for the persistence of the Franciscan charism among various branches of the Christian community after the Reformations of the sixteenth century, including not only the Roman Catholic Church but also robust communities of Franciscans in the Anglican Communion, the Lutheran Church and in various ecumenical organizations.

In a way, we can rightly describe the Franciscan tradition as a reform movement, calling Christians in each time and place to return to the basics of Christian discipleship: living the gospel, following Christ. For this reason, Lent is an especially fitting moment to be guided by the Franciscan charism, challenged by the exemplary models with which the key figures in the tradition provide us, and inspired by the work of the Holy Spirit in our respective sojourns in the desert in order to reform our hearts and minds through prayer, fasting and charity. Despite the movement's titular reference to Francis – *Franciscan* – and indebtedness to his own experience as the inaugural moment of its origins, the Franciscan tradition is much greater than this one individual man from Assisi. The way of the Franciscans is composed of a richly diverse community of women and men who have contributed distinctive insights and models of prayer throughout the centuries. This book is intended to provide readers with an introduction to just a few of the most influential contributors, offering a guide for a Lenten journey of exploration into the manifold expressions of the Franciscan tradition of prayer.

The Franciscan movement's personal foundations and broad appeal

The importance, dignity and value of particularity has been honoured within the Franciscan tradition from its founding. Francis understood his own call to live a renewed Christian life of discipleship as a distinctive vocation, one not at first tied to the founding of formal religious communities of women and men that would grow exponentially even within his lifetime. Instead, he experienced the call from Christ, encounters with lepers and others destitute within the society of his time, and the grace present within all of creation as a personal encounter with the divine. Nobody was more surprised by Francis's profound commitment to Christian conversion than Francis himself, which is registered in the early hagiographic sources of the tradition as shock that anybody would look to his personal spiritual journey as a source of inspiration. In his own words, Francis recounted this surprise at the end of his life when, in his *Testament*, he recalled: 'And after the Lord gave me some brothers, no one showed me what I had to do, but the Most High Himself revealed to me that I should live according to the pattern of the Holy Gospel.'[5] This line speaks volumes of how unprepared the *poverello* – 'the little poor man' of Assisi as he was sometimes known – was for organizing an intentional community of penitents that would form around him.

'No one showed me what I had to do.' No grand plans, no lofty mission statement, no specific ministry or apostolate grounded his vision of the Christian life. While Francis was indeed a reformer, if an unintended one, he never set out to be an innovator. Nevertheless, as Franciscan scholar Bill Short notes:

> The word 'new' recurs frequently in the comments of early observers of the Franciscan movement. Francis himself seemed to many in his day a new kind of Christian, one who did not fit easily within the categories of his day.[6]

His personal vision of a *forma vitae*, or 'way of life', was always oriented towards following Christ more closely and devoting himself more authentically to living the gospel in word and deed. The genius of this simple approach to Christian life focused on the gospel was, perhaps ironically, novel precisely in its simplicity and seeming unoriginality. Many forms of Christian religious life up to that point had focused on strictly defined practices of prayer and spiritual discipline, spaces demarcated within and outside the formal cloister, and religious rules of life that accounted for everything from hierarchical ordering of its members in chapel to, in some cases, the finest details of each day's *horarium* (or 'schedule of life') including when to rise, when to sleep, and the imposition of the evening 'grand silence'. But Francis's way of life, which was occasioned by the particularity of personal conversion, had no such grandiose schemas or contrived regulations. Certainly, with time, more formal structures were incorporated into the daily life of those committed to embracing the Franciscan vision of life. However, the beauty and the challenge of this unpremeditated spiritual reform movement was its open-endedness and general inclusivity. If you felt drawn to following Christ more closely and living the *vita evangelica* ('gospel life'), then the way of the Franciscans might rightly appeal to you.

As a result of the providential appearance of this spiritual movement originating with Francis in the early thirteenth century and attracting thousands of women and men interested in similar personal renewal, diversity and inclusivity were hallmarks of this surprisingly robust community. The early sources recount that the first friars (from the French *frère*, 'brother') came from an array of social backgrounds – noblemen, commoners, a diocesan priest and working-class tradesmen, among others. The appeal of Francis's simple gospel life, commitment to evangelical poverty and prioritization of relationship, especially with the poor and outcast of society, touched the hearts of people across social, ecclesial and geographic divides.

In the Earlier Rule of 1221, which is a document that reflects the continuing emendations of structure into the unplanned *vita evangelica* over the course of more than a decade of living this penitential life, Francis explains that this intentional community that had formed around him was not oriented towards any singular ministry or apostolic task. The Franciscan way allowed for everybody who joined to work diligently and joyfully according to the experience and skills they already had, provided their priorities were always oriented first to God and community. He wrote: 'Let the brothers who know how to work do so and exercise that trade they have learned, provided it is not contrary to the good of their souls and can be performed honestly.'[7] Several years later, with the assistance of the future Pope Gregory IX, the early Franciscan community revised the Rule to state:

> Those brothers to whom the Lord has given the grace of working may work faithfully and devotedly so that, while avoiding idleness, the enemy of the soul, they do not extinguish the Spirit of holy prayer and devotion to which all temporal things must contribute.[8]

What is notable about these instructions on labour within the community is again the emphasis on diversity and inclusivity, limiting the kinds of work a Franciscan can do only in terms of its alignment with the gospel and its subordination to a life of prayer.

Just a few years after Francis began receiving new brothers into this experimental gospel life, Clare of Assisi would become the first woman to commit herself formally to this community. The historical sources recall that on Palm Sunday in the year 1212, Clare left her noble household secretly, accompanied by a companion and with the expressed support of the local bishop, and arrived at the small church of St Mary of the Angels known as the *Portiuncula* ('the little portion') where Francis and his brothers met her and received her into this penitential way of life. Clare asked to have her hair cut to symbolize her conversion to a life of penance. She was then escorted to a local Benedictine convent because she was, at that time, the only woman in this new community. With her reception into the nascent Franciscan community, Clare signalled another chapter of Franciscan inclusivity, not limiting the inspiration of Francis's model of the *vita evangelica* to men alone, but to both men and women. In the years after Francis's death, Clare would compose an original rule for her community of Franciscan sisters – known as the 'Poor Sisters of St Clare', or the 'Poor Clares' as they are called today – thereby making her the first woman in church history to write a religious rule for women. As Regis Armstrong notes: 'The last years of Clare's life were characterized by her struggle to have her vision of religious life approved by the Church.'[9] Clare defied the odds of patriarchal control and benevolent-yet-patronizing oversight by ecclesiastical authorities by insisting that her community of Franciscan women maintain the founding vision of Francis of Assisi's commitment to gospel simplicity, evangelical poverty and the priority of relationship, albeit in a different context shaped by Clare and her sisters' embrace of the religious cloister, which means they lived a monastic life and rarely left their convent. Not long before her death in 1253, Pope Innocent IV finally granted her wish, bestowing pontifical approval on her distinctively Franciscan rule.

Clare's personal spiritual journey and its influence on the particular manner of life shared among her sisters bears witness to yet
another form of Franciscan particularity.

In addition to the formal communities of Franciscan men and
women who professed religious vows to live the *vita evangelica* –
the Franciscan friars and the Poor Clare Sisters respectively –
there was also a third community that was drawn to Francis's vision and model of Christian life. Emerging early in the nascent
Franciscan movement, a category of lay penitents known as the
'brothers and sisters of penance' sought to deepen their own experience of gospel life and looked to Francis as their exemplar. Initially, this group was composed of women and men who did not
desire to enter into a formal religious community such as that of
the friars or Poor Clares, but nevertheless wished to align themselves with this penitential reform movement. Like the brothers
and sisters who eventually professed religious vows, these laypeople came from all walks of life; their unity amid diversity was
made possible by a shared commitment to living the holy gospel
of our Lord Jesus Christ. In time, some of these laypeople formed
intentional communities of apostolic life, establishing congrega-
tions of men and women religious who professed vows and served
the Church and society in a manner inspired by Francis and Clare
of Assisi. In effect, what began as a singular grouping, known as
the 'brothers and sisters of penance', eventually became two related but distinct expressions of Franciscan life that continue to
thrive to this day: the laypeople known now as Secular Franciscans or the Third Order of St Francis, and the vowed religious
known as the Third Order Regular.

Throughout this book, we will come to know better some of the
key figures in all three categories, or 'orders' as the three branches
of the Franciscan family are officially known. Over the centuries,
some people have lamented that the Franciscan movement is so
broad and its manifold iterations so diverse. Such critics have focused on the heterogeneity of the Franciscan tradition as a sign of
weakness or lack of unity. However, I approach this historical and
spiritual phenomenon from a different perspective. I believe the

breadth and, subsequently, the depth of the Franciscan tradition reflects the work of God's grace in all corners of society and the Church, which bespeaks the richness and fecundity of the originating vision expressed in the personal experience of Francis's own ongoing conversion. Dating back to the earliest years of the Franciscan movement, there has always been broad appeal and plenty of room for particularity in the lived expression of the founding charism, rooted as it was in the simple and personal commitment to walk in the footprints of Jesus Christ. Because the scope of the Franciscan movement had never been limited to a singular or exclusive expression, but has reflected and continues to reflect a broad range of modalities, so too prayer in the Franciscan tradition can never be reduced to merely one style or form. As we have seen, diversity has always been a central characteristic of the Franciscan tradition, which represents both its greatest blessing and its greatest challenge.

The diversity of Franciscan prayer

Franciscan scholar Timothy Johnson keenly observes that 'there is no single, uniform Franciscan manner of prayer because there is a plurality of unique Franciscan witnesses, whose desire to live an evangelical life fostered as many individual expressions of prayer as people committed to the Poor Christ'.[10] While all the major contributors and models of Franciscan prayer can, in some sense, point back to Francis and Clare of Assisi as their primary inspirations and guides, the assortment of prayers, practices and approaches to the spiritual life present in the history of Franciscan spirituality offers modern spiritual seekers a broad range of resources and insight.

This can be a frustrating reality for some people. For those interested in a one-stop, simple primer on 'Franciscan prayer', disappointment is waiting around the corner. Just as there has never been one singular form of work or ministerial apostolate associated with the Franciscan movement, so too there is no singular, top-down method of prayer. This can be contrasted, for example, with the sixteenth-century tradition of Ignatius Loyola, who not only deliberately founded a congregation of apostolic life – the Society of Jesus, better known simply as 'the Jesuits' – but also wrote a clear and direct programme for prayer known as 'the Spiritual Exercises'. As Gemma Simmonds notes, while the text itself is not inherently edifying in the way that an individual might pick up a collection of poetry or a spiritual classic to find personal insight to aid one's prayer life, it is nevertheless extraordinarily detailed and programmatic, written 'principally for those accompanying others in their spiritual life, and it is thus somewhat technical'.[11] In other words, Ignatius clearly and deliberately developed an explicit method of prayer and programme for instructing others in that approach. References to 'Ignatian spirituality' inevitably begin and end with the founder of the Jesuits and the way he instructed his followers to pray.

But this is not the case in the Franciscan tradition.

While Francis of Assisi is indisputably (if also, by his own admittance, unwittingly) the founder of the Franciscan movement, he did not leave a clear and direct method of prayer or programme of instruction. In fact, so committed was he to creating the space necessary for those inspired by his model of Christian living to discover their own meaningful paths to prayer, he actively discouraged his followers from strictly imitating him. One early biography tells the story of a friar known as 'Brother John the Simple', who so admired Francis that he sought to imitate everything he said and did.

Whenever Saint Francis stayed in some place to meditate, simple John would immediately repeat and copy whatever gestures or movements the saint made. If he spat, John would spit too, if he coughed, he would cough as well, sighing or sobbing along with him. If the saint lifted up his hands to heaven, John would raise his too, and he watched him intently as a model, turning himself into a copy of all his actions. The saint noticed this, and once asked him why he did those things. He replied: 'I promised to do everything you do. It is dangerous for me to leave anything out.' The saint delighted in this pure simplicity, *but gently told him not to do this anymore.*[12]

Also, near the end of his life, the same source recounts how Francis on his deathbed said to his brother friars: 'I have done what is mine; may Christ teach you what is yours!'[13] As the historian André Vauchez explains:

> From the life and writings of Francis we get a new definition of what it means to be religious: it ceases being a separate category, distinct from the profane, and becomes a commitment to embracing all aspects of one's personality and life.[14]

Francis understood that the spiritual life is a distinctly personal journey, not one that was travelled alone – for he came to realize over time how central the prioritization of relationship is to Christian discipleship – but one that could never be completely fulfilled by a 'one size fits all' approach to prayer. In this way, Francis's outlook anticipated the deceptively simple yet profoundly insightful observation of the twentieth-century Trappist monk Thomas Merton, himself deeply inspired by the Franciscan tradition: 'For me to be a saint means to be myself. Therefore the problem of sanctity and salvation is in fact the problem of finding out who I am and of discovering my true self.'[15]

Although this sense of breadth of Franciscan approaches to prayer may be an understandable source of frustration for some, it is also a wonderful aspect of Franciscan spirituality. The tradition is rich, diverse, inclusive and varied. There are some key themes that appear throughout the range of approaches to prayer over the generations and among its main contributors – such as the centrality of God's incarnation and Christ's crucifixion, the importance of creation, the significance of evangelical poverty, and the prioritization of relationship – but diversity is truly a Franciscan hallmark. Given the simplicity of the founding charism – the desire to more authentically live the gospel and follow Christ – there is a distinctive openness to Franciscan prayer that is not often found in other Christian spiritual traditions, associated as so many of them are with an individual founder or charismatic figure. The array of spiritual texts, styles of prayer and methods for contemplation contained within the canon of the eight-centuries-old tradition offers something for everyone at each stage of her or his life.

This book is designed to introduce readers to this broad Franciscan tradition, inviting spiritual seekers to sample the range of approaches to, and perspectives on, deepening one's relationship to God, one another and all creation. This provides a unique opportunity for modern spiritual seekers. While the approaches, writings or insights of this or that individual contributor to the Franciscan tradition may not appeal to you, everybody is bound to find something within the collective wisdom of the Franciscan movement that speaks to her or his heart and soul. Furthermore, as time goes on and personal tastes or life experiences shift, there are sure to be other approaches within this robust and expansive tradition to aid one's prayer at other moments in life.

Overview of the book

This prayer journey through Lent explores the diverse landscape that is the world of Franciscan spirituality. Each of the following six chapters traverses the context and content of a major contributor to the tradition. We begin our journey in Chapter 1 with Francis of Assisi, the founder and namesake of the spiritual movement. His approach to prayer can be summarized by two 'poles' or complementary foci upon which stands his spirituality: an emphasis on the importance of solitude on the one hand and, on the other, the transformation of one's entire life into a form of 'living prayer' exemplified by deepening one's ongoing relationship to God, others and all of creation.

In Chapter 2, the wisdom of Clare of Assisi, the first female Franciscan and the rightfully named co-founder of the tradition, guides us. While sharing some fundamental gospel principles with

Francis – such as the love of Christ, the embrace of evangelical poverty, and so on – Clare nevertheless leaves us with unique contributions to prayer and spirituality all her own. In particular, the way Clare understands contemplation and offers something of a method of prayer provides us with an important resource in the Franciscan tradition.

The next chapter focuses on one of the better-known contributors to the Franciscan tradition: Bonaventure of Bagnoregio, the extraordinary theologian, Doctor of the Church, former Minister General of the Franciscan Order, as well as bishop and cardinal. A contemporary of Clare's, Bonaventure offers yet another approach to our understanding of 'Franciscan contemplation', which emphasizes the presence of God in all creation and calls for a transformation of the one praying to see the world anew. Contemplation, in Bonaventure's understanding, is not limited to moments we set aside in quiet alone, but is something that can potentially be experienced at all times and places, making contemplation a call to what the twentieth-century theologian Karl Rahner famously called 'everyday mysticism'.

Chapter 4 introduces the thirteenth-century lay Franciscan mystic Angela of Foligno. A member of what today is known as the 'Secular Franciscan Order', Angela was born a generation after Francis and Clare and became widely renowned in her own time as a mystic and spiritual guide. While not as well known as Francis, Clare or Bonaventure, admiration for Angela's powerful mystical experiences and spiritual writing has led to her continued relevance, which was affirmed by her canonization in 2013 by Pope Francis. A mother, wife and mystic, she offers us unique insights from a Franciscan perspective on Christ and creation, providing us with yet another resource on our prayer journey through Lent.

The next chapter focuses on the Franciscan philosopher and theologian John Duns Scotus, who is oftentimes remembered for his esoteric and deeply complex scholarly treatises, such as the logical framework for what would become the Catholic dogma of the immaculate conception. Despite his reputation for challenging academic writing, Scotus was a deeply prayerful and spiritual Franciscan friar whose reflections on God and humanity have shaped spiritual luminaries over the centuries, including the Jesuit poet Gerard Manley Hopkins and the Trappist monk Thomas Merton, to name just two. Scotus gives us renewed insight into prayer in the Franciscan tradition, as his own distinctive contributions make clear.

Finally, the last chapter focuses on three Franciscans who are not as well known as those already explored in this book. Jacopone da Todi, a medieval Franciscan friar and poet, offers us a different medium for spiritual reflection through his inspirational *Lauds*. Catherine of Bologna, a fifteenth-century Poor Clare sister, provides us with an original guide to contemplative prayer, which frames our prayer life within the context of defending ourselves against sin and temptation in order to better follow Christ. And, finally, Solanus Casey, a twentieth-century American Capuchin Franciscan friar, directs our attention to the importance of translating our prayer lives into Christlike action in the world.

Each chapter is written to be self-contained and can, therefore, be read in any order. Additionally, every chapter concludes with a few questions for reflection or group discussion. It is my hope that the key Franciscan figures presented in this book offer each reader an engaging entry point into the inspiring and broad tradition of Franciscan prayer. During this season of penance and preparation for Easter, may you find yourself renewed by journeying along the way of the Franciscans towards a deeper experience of prayer and a closer relationship with God, others and all creation.

Questions for reflection or discussion

1 For some people, the simplicity of the Franciscan tradition with its emphasis on the gospel as the guiding principle may be as challenging as it is inspiring. How do you relate to the simplicity of Franciscan spirituality? What role does the gospel play in your prayer journey?

2 Unlike many other spiritual traditions within Christianity, the Franciscan way of prayer is notably diverse. What is appealing about the range of approaches? What do you find challenging about such diversity within one tradition?

3 The beauty of the Franciscan tradition is that, despite its distinctive ties to one medieval Italian man, it remains ever timely and appealing in each new age. How might you embody the Franciscan way of prayer in your own life, time and place?

1

Francis of Assisi: Solitude and relationship

Despite the lore that surrounds canonized saints, especially widely beloved figures such as St Francis of Assisi, it is important to remember that these venerated women and men were just like you and me. Francesco di Bernardone entered the world sometime around the year 1182 neither a sinner nor a saint, but a person created in the image and likeness of a loving God. Like all of us, he sinned and broke relationships, thought of himself at times before thinking of others, and undoubtedly made decisions that he later regretted (the early Franciscan sources recount several such instances). But, also like you and me, Francis was created inherently good and expressed love and generosity in numerous ways to friends, family and strangers alike. While it is accurate to say that Francis was *neither* a sinner nor a saint, it is also just as true to state that during his lifetime he was *both* a sinner and a saint, for that is what we all are in our journeys of faith in this life.

It is important to state this simple yet easily forgotten fact from the outset because too many Christians are often quick to dismiss the examples of canonized saints as practically unattainable on account of our collective tendency to place highly regarded holy women and men on pedestals. They are revered from a distance but not often viewed as credible models for everyday, contemporary, ordinary Christian living. And yet Francis was as ordinary as one could be, and remembering that may help us to see the timeliness and relevance of his own insights about prayer for our lives.

Francis experienced a series of events early in his young adulthood that came together in such a way as to open his eyes to a reality previously veiled from him by his relatively affluent upbringing and comfortable social status. The son of a wealthy cloth merchant, Francis lived in the thirteenth-century Umbrian town of Assisi in what is today the country of Italy. As a matter of birth, he did not have noble status (something his first female follower, Clare of Assisi, did enjoy), though he sought to attain a higher place in society for himself and his family by becoming a successful knight in battle defending his hometown. Despite his best intentions to achieve acclaim and status by means of demonstrating military prowess, Francis was not a great soldier. During his first – and, ultimately, last – foray into battle in the inter-city conflict with the neighbouring town of Perugia, Francis was swiftly captured in November 1202 and held as a prisoner of war for about a year. It was during his time as a prisoner that, according to contemporary biographers and scholars, Francis first came to an awareness of the need to change his manner of life. As Franciscan historian Dominic Monti describes it, Francis's 'long confinement had created an opportunity for him to reevaluate his direction in life. Although he returned to his former work and amusements, they no longer offered the same fulfillment.'[1] From about 1204 to 1206, Francis embarked on what would become a lifelong experience of conversion shaped by his dedication to a 'life of penance'. He began taking time to be alone in prayer and reflection, and discerned how exactly God was calling him to live his Christian life in a new way.

It would take time for Francis to gain clarity about what God had in store for him. Later in life, Francis would credit divine intervention in helping him to realize that Christian discipleship required prioritizing relationship above all else in a manner that reflected Jesus's own ministry and teaching. At first, as his earliest biographer Thomas of Celano put it, Francis was changed 'in mind but not in body'. The biographer goes on to note: 'he retired for a short time from the tumult and business of the world and was anxious to keep Jesus Christ in his inmost self.'[2] Francis was nominally committed to living a more dedicated life of Christian discipleship, but this was at first made manifest only in his personal devotional practice. Initially, Francis lived as a public penitent, donning the simple peasant clothes of one professing to live a life of personal conversion and penance. In time, he came to engage in more overt actions of charity and kindness, selling cloth from his father's store and giving the proceeds to a local church or beggar. Eventually, as the years progressed, he moved outside the confines of the familiar Assisi community he had known from birth in order to embrace a more precarious existence at the periphery of society and in solidarity with the marginalized, especially the poor and the lepers.

It was in this period of his life that the centrality of relationship in Christian life came into greater relief for Francis. It was among the marginalized and voiceless that Francis began to experience God in a new way. And it was the experience of breaking with his own social class and comfortable upbringing in order to embrace a more permanent itinerant lifestyle that marked the most clearly recognizable moment of his continuing experience of conversion to gospel life. As we saw in the Introduction, Francis recalled on his deathbed that this experience of those deemed 'less-than' or 'other' by society and the Church at the time was what most profoundly influenced his desire to live a life of penance. As Franciscan historian Michael Cusato keenly notes, in that encounter with the experience of the marginalized – especially the 'lepers outside the city of Assisi' who were 'men and women whom he had always considered abhorrent and of no consequence . . . Francis had his eyes open onto a whole world of suffering humanity which, up to that time, he had been socialized by the values of Assisi to ignore, avoid, and despise as repugnant and useless blots upon social life.'³ Francis's encounter with the poor of his time radically shifted his world view and forced him to see the inherent relational quality of Christian discipleship.

That Francis could not live an authentic Christian life alone, but must always be mindful of encountering the other, was further emphasized in his experience of being confronted with men and women inspired by his evangelical awakening. Despite his initial understanding of his faith journey as a solo venture, women and men were drawn to him, captivated by his public witness and life choices. He had to grapple with the reality that God was using him as an instrument of inspiration and guidance for others who likewise felt the stirring of the Holy Spirit in their hearts and desired to embrace a life of penance like the *poverello*. The more Francis surrendered to the will of God over his own initial desire to live the gospel as something of a 'lone ranger', the more relationship became the central focus of his spirituality and prayer life.

The centrality of Christ

The heart of the Franciscan way of life (*vita evangelica*) is living after the pattern of the holy gospel by walking in the footprints of Jesus Christ.[4] Recognizing the central place of divine–human relationship that occasioned the eternal Word's becoming flesh in the incarnation, Francis was drawn to the kenotic model of humility and poverty exhibited by Christ. We see in his writings this emphasis on God's self-emptying as the emblematic mode of being in the world. Tying together this kenosis of God with the poverty of Christ, Francis writes in chapter six of the Rule for the Franciscan friars:

> Let the brothers not make anything their own, neither house, nor place, nor anything at all. As pilgrims and strangers in this world, serving the Lord in poverty and humility, let them go seeking alms with confidence, and they should not be ashamed because, for our sakes, *our Lord made Himself poor in this world*. This is that sublime height of most exalted poverty which has made you, my most beloved brothers, heirs and kings of the Kingdom of Heaven, poor in temporal things but exalted in virtue. Let this be your portion which leads into the land of the living. Giving yourselves totally to this, beloved brothers, never seek anything else under heaven for the name of our Lord Jesus Christ.[5]

Poverty for Francis was not simply an end in itself but a means to becoming more like Christ in terms of entering into relationship more deeply with God, one's neighbours and all of creation.

Gospel poverty is always tied to the incarnation, which for Francis most fully symbolized God's desire to draw near to humanity in creation.

This same pattern was evident in Francis's strong devotion to the Eucharist, which also occupied a particularly central place in the *poverello*'s own spirituality. In the Middle Ages, it became commonplace for Catholics not only to receive the Eucharist at liturgy but also to spend time in prayer before the Blessed Sacrament in the places where it was reserved in churches outside the context of the Mass. In a letter to the entire order, Francis wrote that the friars should not only adore the eucharistic elements or receive them with devotion. Instead, they are to recall the continuing kenotic – a term meaning 'self-emptying' from the Greek – action of God in the celebration of the Eucharist, which should serve yet again as a model for Franciscan life and prayer. He writes:

> What wonderful majesty! What stupendous condescension! O sublime humility! O humble sublimity! That the Lord of the whole universe, God and the Son of God, should humble himself like this and hide under the form of a little piece of bread, for our salvation. Look at God's condescension, my brothers, and pour out your hearts before him. Humble yourselves that you may be exalted by him. Keep back nothing of yourselves for yourselves, so that he who has given himself wholly to you may receive you wholly.[6]

These illustrations of Francis's writings on the significance of the incarnation as the model for Christian living – particularly in terms of embracing humility and evangelical poverty – echo what is seen in the New Testament writings of Paul. Take, for example, the ancient christological hymn in the Letter to the Philippians:

> Let each of you look not to your own interests, but to the interests of others. Let the same mind be in you that was in Christ Jesus,

who, though he was in the form of God,
    did not regard equality with God
    as something to be exploited,
but emptied himself,
    taking the form of a slave,
    being born in human likeness.
And being found in human form,
    he humbled himself
    and became obedient to the point of death –
    even death on a cross.
Therefore God also highly exalted him
    and gave him the name that is above every
      name,
so that at the name of Jesus
    every knee should bend,
    in the heaven and on earth and under the
      earth,
and every tongue should confess
    that Jesus Christ is Lord,
    to the glory of God the Father.
(Philippians 2.4–11).

One can see the resonances immediately present between the self-emptying incarnational spirituality Francis exhorted those who followed him to adopt and the Pauline theology of divine kenosis.

This sense of the importance of the incarnation is found beyond Francis's own writings and witnessed in the early testimony of those attesting to have known Francis personally. Such is the case in an early remembrance about Francis's view of Christmas.

For blessed Francis held the Nativity of the Lord in greater reverence than any other of the Lord's solemnities. For although the Lord may have accomplished our salvation in his other solemnities, nevertheless, once He was born to us, as blessed Francis would say, it was certain that we would be saved.[7]

Francis understood that the humility of the incarnation was one half of the two-sided coin of God's salvific action. The other side of the coin was the Passion, death and resurrection of the Lord, which also plays a key role in Francis's approach to prayer. His early biographer, Thomas of Celano, wrote: 'The humility of the incarnation and the charity of the passion occupied his memory particularly, to the extent that he wanted to think of hardly anything else.'[8] Furthermore, Franciscan scholar Norbert Nguyên-Van-Khanh explains:

> In reality, there are not two different subjects: the incarnation and the passion. For Francis, the passion is situated along a line that leads logically from the incarnation; it is a consequence of the fact that the Son of the Father accepts the human condition to the very end. The incarnation is the movement of descent; it is not a static situation that ends in the passion and death. Therefore, in the mind of Francis, the passion is intimately linked to the birth.[9]

This incarnational vision tied to the Passion of the Lord is also never divorced from a soundly Trinitarian theological understanding of the God to whom Francis prayed. Since prayer for Francis became increasingly understood in relational terms, it is not surprising that he would name God in the triune manner of orthodox Christian theology. For example, in the so-called 'earlier Rule' (*Regula non bullata*), believed to have been completed around 1221, Francis includes a prayer near the end of the text in which God is addressed as Trinity:

> All-powerful, most holy, Almighty and supreme God, Holy and just Father, Lord King of heaven and earth we thank You for Yourself for through Your holy will and through Your only Son with the Holy Spirit You have created everything spiritual and corporal and, after making us in Your image and likeness, You placed us in paradise.[10]

Francis of Assisi's sense of prayer was an address and form of communication with his Creator, Redeemer and Sanctifier, but also a constant return to the model of authentic human life and love. Paraphrasing the classic patristic formula *lex orandi, lex credendi* ('the law of praying is the law of believing'), which refers to the tradition of mutual influence of worship and doctrine, the Franciscan scholar Michael Blastic suggests:

> One can expand on this conviction with another formula, 'forma vivendi forma orandi,' which suggests the mutual relationship between life and prayer, that is the pattern and meaning of one's life is articulated in the form of one's prayer, and vice versa.[11]

From his writings and the early sources, we can conclude that Francis's approach to prayer extended beyond a sense of two-way dialogue to include a pattern for his way of life. What exactly that way of life looked like can be seen in his instructions to his followers about the importance of prayer and the various modes it may take.

Francis's guidance on prayer

As mentioned in the Introduction, unlike some other religious traditions such as Ignatius Loyola's concentrated, step-by-step instructions for prayer in his Spiritual Exercises, Francis of Assisi's guidance for those who wish to follow his example of prayer and devotion is more diffuse. It is true to think of Francis's writings as occasional and unsystematic. Nevertheless, taken as a whole, they offer constructive clues for what we might describe generally as Francis's 'instructions on prayer'. For the sake of brevity, we will look at four such instructions: the need to prioritize prayer, reverence for the Eucharist, the importance of solitude, and the call to immerse oneself in sacred Scripture. All four of these themes are aimed at leading those inspired by Francis's pattern of life (*forma vitae*) to move from simply 'saying prayers' to becoming a living prayer.

The importance of prayer

First, prayer enters early into the formal vision of the Franciscan way of life in the Rule. After the brief introductory section where Francis announces the pattern of life is simply the gospel of Jesus Christ and then outlines the logistics of accepting would-be friars into the community, Francis offers a chapter on prayer, fasting and the general way the brothers are to live in the world.[12] It should come as no surprise, given the role that hierarchical church leaders in Rome played in the formation of this officially approved *Rule* for the friars, that the Divine Office (the daily prayers of religious communities, largely consisting of the psalms) required by the Church for the friar clerics would make an appearance. Yet, Francis is also accommodating for those who may be uneducated or illiterate, permitting them to pray a prescribed number of Our Fathers. One may glean from this inclusion that, although not everyone could be expected to pray the formal Liturgy of Hours, all the brothers in community are expected to pray in community. Unlike the demarcation in traditional monastic communities of women and men religious who live in a strict cloister between so-called 'choir monks' (usually the ordained) and 'lay monks', whose responsibilities largely centred on manual labour, Francis affirmed a more egalitarian vision of fraternal life and activity grounded in prayer.

The importance of grounding one's life and activity in prayer is seen especially in Francis's explicit instruction on labour in chapter five of the Rule:

> Those brothers to whom the Lord has given the grace of working *may work faithfully and devotedly* so that, while avoiding idleness, the enemy of the soul, *they do not extinguish the Spirit of holy prayer and devotion* to which all temporal things must contribute.[13]

That the work of the brothers, however conceived in terms of explicit apostolic ministry or manual labour, should always be subordinate to one's individual and collective 'spirit of prayer and devotion' attests to the importance of prayer in Francis's vision of gospel life. Francis again reiterates this prioritization when, in a now-famous letter to Anthony of Padua, Francis gives permission to teach theology to the brothers: 'I am pleased that you teach sacred theology to the brothers providing that, as is contained in the Rule, you "do not extinguish the Spirit of prayer and devotion" during study of this kind.'[14]

In something of a departure from the Benedictine tradition's emphasis on maintaining a balanced life of *ora et labora*, prayer and work, Francis tilts the scales towards prayer. While work is important, it is, for Francis, never more important than perseverance in the spiritual life. For Francis, prayer was understood as both a continual and a communal experience, even when one's activity was an effort in solitude. The sense of continual prayer – the continuing communication with God throughout all facets of life both in the more explicit *ora* as well as during all other *labora* – is seen in Francis's 'Later Admonition and Exhortation', in which we read:

> Let us love God, therefore, and adore Him with a pure heart and a pure mind, because He Who seeks this above all things has said: True adorers adore the Father in Spirit and Truth. For all who adore Him must adore Him in the Spirit of truth. And day and night let us direct praises and prayers to Him saying: Our Father, Who art in heaven . . . for we should pray always and not become weary.[15]

And yet this was also a deeply communal dimension of Francis's vision of gospel life. As Michael Blastic has observed, among Francis's authentic writings only one is voiced in the first person singular, that of the 'Prayer before the Crucifix', which reads: 'Most High, glorious God, enlighten the darkness of my heart and give me true faith, certain hope, and perfect charity, sense and knowledge, Lord, that I may carry out Your holy and true command.'[16] What remains of Francis's prayers assume a collective voice, representing 'the voice of the brotherhood at work'.[17] Prayer is always a communal experience, one that extends beyond the individual petitioner or adorer of God to include the community gathered locally or the communion of saints more broadly.

Reverence for the Eucharist

Second, Francis frequently reflects on the Eucharist and the importance that the brothers approach the Blessed Sacrament in a spirit of prayerful reverence. Francis's personal devotion to the celebration of the Mass, his admiration of the office of the ministerial priesthood (as distinct from particular *priests* who, as Francis noted with realistic acquiescence, are as finite and sinful as everybody else), and reverence for the Eucharist are commonly found throughout his writings. From the beginning of his ongoing conversion around 1206 to his death on 3 October 1226, his writings do not include extensive instruction on the role of liturgical prayer in the life of the community apart from the clerical daily office.[18] This is very likely reflective of the shift in friar demographics. In the beginning, those following Francis's nascent form of life represented a diverse mixture of backgrounds and experiences. Towards the end of Francis's short life, a larger number of ordained priests began entering the community, which shifted the availability of the sacraments within Franciscan houses. Correspondingly, the later texts of Francis tend to include references to the celebration of the Eucharist and a call for increased participation in the Mass and reverence for the Blessed Sacrament on the part of his followers.

The importance of solitude

Third, the incorporation of a part-time eremitical (that is, living like a hermit) experience into the broader pattern of life was an important dimension of Francis's own spirituality and approach to prayer.[19] He believed in the need for the brothers to reconnect with God in an attentive and deliberate way, which was demonstrated in his own practice of regularly retreating to hermitages and quiet places. Though his general emphasis on relationship with others by meeting them where they are in the streets and villages of the world through a commitment to itinerant ministry was central to the Franciscan Rule, he nevertheless went to the trouble of composing a short 'Rule

for Hermitages'. This unique text is worth citing at length, for it reveals at once the importance of experiencing and preserving solitude
and the communal-fraternal dimension of lived Franciscan prayer.

> Not more than three or at most four friars should go together
> to a hermitage to lead a religious life there. Two of these should
> act as mothers, with the other two, or the other one, as their
> children. The mothers are to lead the life of Martha; the other
> two, the life of Mary . . . The friars who are mothers must be
> careful to stay away from outsiders and in obedience to their
> minister keep their sons away from outsiders, so that no one
> can speak to them. The friars who are sons are not to speak to
> anyone except their mother or their minister, when he visits
> them, with God's blessing. Now and then, the sons should
> exchange places with the mothers, according to whatever
> arrangement seems best suited for the time. But they should
> all be careful to observe what has been laid down for them,
> eagerly and zealously.[20]

Striking is the freedom with which Francis invokes as instructive
for the brothers the maternal imagery and the model of Martha and
Mary from the Gospels. Though not often well known or acknowledged by modern Franciscans, scholars have nonetheless noted the
distinctive contribution that Francis's vision of non-dominating
governance within the fraternity, frequently conveyed in feminine
imagery, has made to Christian spirituality.[21] Solitude was not only
an important ingredient in gospel life for Francis himself but was
intended to be a mainstay of Franciscan prayer more generally by
offering an opportunity for small communities to care for one another and provide the space for ongoing, deep encounters with the
divine.[22]

Becoming a person of Scripture

Fourth, Francis's way of Christian living and approach to prayer
were deeply tied to sacred Scripture. Though the early sources recall
Francis's self-deprecating identification as an *idiota*, or unlearned

person, Francis most certainly knew how to read and write. It can be difficult for modern people who are used to mass-produced paper, living centuries after the invention of the printing press, to appreciate how important the written word was in Francis's time. Oftentimes, the materials needed to write a copy of a biblical book or the prayers for the Mass were difficult to acquire and expensive. Unlike our bound liturgical books and Bibles today, Scripture was often copied out on a variety of pages. These pages, usually unbound, had the tendency (as most loose papers do) to become scattered and lost. This even happened in churches. Francis was very concerned about the way these particles of Scripture were cared for (or, more accurately, not cared for). He was almost obsessed with making sure that all pieces of Scripture were well taken care of and treated with respect and dignity. In a letter addressed to the entire order, Francis shares his vision of the importance of caring for Scripture in a command that all friars should go out of their way to gather, protect and venerate even the most seemingly insignificant scriptural texts. He wrote:

Because whoever belongs to God hears the words of God, we who are more especially charged with divine responsibilities must not only listen to and do what the Lord says but also care for the vessels and other liturgical objects that contain His holy words in order to impress on ourselves the sublimity of our Creator and our subjection to Him. I, therefore, admonish all my brothers and encourage them in Christ to venerate, as best as they can, the divine written words wherever they find them. If they are not well kept or are carelessly thrown around in some place, let them gather them up and preserve them, inasmuch as it concerns them, honoring in the words the Lord Who spoke them. For many things are made holy by the words of God and the sacrament of the altar is celebrated in the power of the words of Christ.[23]

Francis did not see in the word of God some removed and abstract sense of God's presence, but recognized the truly intimate and life-giving quality of Scripture. We see this most strongly in the assertion that Francis makes prior to instructing his brothers to collect these pieces of Scripture, when he explains that it is Scripture that allows us to 'impress on ourselves the greatness of our Creator'. His instruction to his followers was no mere 'housekeeping' task, but a sign that he recognized God's 'spirit and life' communicated through Scripture.[24]

Though he does not outline any particular programme or method of reading and meditating on Scripture (for example, a formal process of *lectio divina*), Francis does communicate in subtler ways the necessity of living by the word of God. This is seen in his emphasis on the daily office prayed in community, as well as through the extraordinary frequency with which he cites the Scriptures in his own writings, Rules and prayers. St Bonaventure, in his first biography of St Francis, describes the unique way in which the poor man from Assisi was able to understand the meaning of Scripture such that he astounded even the most learned and wise scholars of the day.

Unflagging zeal for prayer
with a continual exercise of virtue
had led the man of God to such serenity of mind
    that,
although he had no expertise in Sacred Scripture
    through learning,
his intellect, nevertheless
enlightened by the splendor of eternal light,
probed the depths of Scripture
with remarkable incisiveness.
For his genius, pure and unstained,
Penetrated hidden mysteries,
and where the knowledge of teachers stands out-
    side,
the passion of the lover entered.
Whenever he read the Sacred Books,
and something struck his mind

he imprinted it tenaciously on his memory,
because he did not grasp in vain
what his attentive mind heard,
for he would mull over it
with affection and constant devotion.[25]

Francis's memorization of, reflection on and constant reference to sacred Scripture led to his being imbued with the very narrative of God's self-disclosure. In turn, he was inspired to draw on passages from the Bible, especially the psalms, to compose his own psalmody and prayers. This is seen most clearly in his creative *Office of the Passion*, which was modelled on the personal devotional offices commonly found among monastic communities.[26] Here, Francis weaves together various psalms from the Hebrew Bible with his own devotional interludes and psalm-like additions. The importance of Scripture in prayer was not limited to Francis's private devotional life alone, but was seen by him as an essential element of evangelical life.

Becoming a 'living prayer'

St Augustine of Hippo (d. 430) famously remarks at various points in his expansive corpus that God is the one who is closer to us than we are to ourselves.[27] This experience of divine immanence, of the presence of God among and within creation, was the keystone of Francis's whole approach to prayer, though it is safe to say that he did not realize this overnight. It is always important to remember the lifelong experience of continuing conversion when calling to mind Francis's spirituality and form of prayer. As noted earlier, he began his renewed commitment to Christian living in early young adulthood with what we might anachronistically call a 'literal approach' to discipleship. His focus was on the externals of affective religiosity, such as attending Mass and physically rebuilding churches. The increasing number of relational encounters – the living among lepers, the unsolicited brothers and sisters, the reception of Clare, the protection and approval of the clerical hierarchy, the embrace of the Muslim Sultan, the increasing awakening to his part in the cosmic family of creation, and so on – shifted, over time, the *poverello's* vision of prayer. In the beginning, as Thomas of Celano notes, Francis of Assisi was one who merely 'said' prayers but, over time, became a 'living prayer'.[28]

If prayer is, as we might all agree, always a form of 'communication with God', then we are in some sense always praying because God is always already present to us (again, Augustine's insight about God's immanence and proximity to us). It is in a sense a form of hubris to think that we can simply 'turn on' or 'turn off' the prayer channel, as if we had the ability to select when God is or is not able to receive our missives. In truth, not only what we say or think, but how we act, what we prioritize, how we love, how we care for one another, and so on, all combine to *communicate* something to the God who is at all times nearer to us than we are to ourselves. In commenting on Francis's Rule, Blastic explains:

> It describes an experience of prayer and life without dichotomy, and without separating out the realms of the sacred and the secular . . . This world becomes the location for prayer, the place for returning all things to God, and this is situated in the context of faith in the Trinity who acts in history as creator and savior.

He continues, noting the way we must consider a summation of Francis's whole life of prayer: 'Prayer is rooted firmly in the ordinary activity of life in terms of love and service, and it is expressed here in terms of praise, adoration, and glory.'[29]

Long before Ignatius and his successors in the Society of Jesus popularized the expression 'finding God in all things', Francis of Assisi's understanding and experience of prayer was precisely this form of ordinary mysticism. He came to realize in time that the words said in the divine office, the community's participation in the celebration of the Eucharist, and charitable acts of love and mercy were not as distinct as one might first assume. Instead, prayer for Francis was always a journey of growing more deeply in relationship with God and neighbour, including his non-human neighbours in the great family of creation. There is no explicit strategy or instruction manual proposed as a means to achieve this mystical awareness. And yet, Francis's own narrative of lifelong conversion and his model for how to prioritize the elements of one's life – never extinguish the spirit of prayer and devotion, embrace regular solitude, and so on – provide us with a pattern of life, a guide for our own journeys, a series of points for reflection. The goal of prayer (if prayer can ever be said to have a *goal*) in the Franciscan tradition, put simply, is nothing more than for each of us, in our own ways and in our own contexts, to become more and more a living prayer.

Questions for reflection or discussion

1 Francis of Assisi's conversion began with his experience of seeking an individual path towards sanctity, but soon God put others in his spiritual path such that he came to recognize the centrality of relationship in the Christian life. What role do the relationships in your life play in your experience of prayer? How do you experience the blessings and challenges of family or community life?

2 While Francis was profoundly drawn to the mystery of the tri-une God, Christ also stands at the centre of his life of prayer. How do you understand Jesus Christ? What place does Christ have in your prayer?

3 Solitude was an important aspect of the spiritual life for Francis, as was the growing awareness of his entire life as a form of prayer or communication with God. How do you incorporate solitude into your spiritual practice? What is your understanding of prayer, and how might Francis's model to 'become a living prayer' challenge or support your understanding?

2

Clare of Assisi: Poverty, contemplation and the cross

Clare of Assisi is often portrayed as the 'woman behind the man' in the hagiographical telling of the early Franciscan movement. And while it is correct to say that she was the first woman to join Francis of Assisi's nascent penitential community (she entered on Palm Sunday 1212 at around the age of 17), her significant role in shaping what would come to be known as the Franciscan movement and its spirituality has been largely overlooked through the centuries. This oversight is likely due in part to the patriarchal presuppositions of historiography (how history is written) that were commonplace until recently. Fortunately, in recent decades, scholarship has begun to catch up to reality, presenting a rich tapestry of detail about and insight into the identity, role and legacy of Clare.[1]

Unlike Francis, who was the son of a comfortably successful cloth merchant in Assisi but whose status was nevertheless of common origin, Clare came from a family of some nobility and high social standing. In the regional civil war that pitted the *minores* (commoners) against the *maiores* (aristocracy) in the village of Assisi, Francis's family was part of the uprising of the former, while Clare's family fled to the safety of a nearby town for a time because they belonged to the latter social class. This early distinction between the two founders of the Franciscan movement would not be the only difference between them. In addition to gender identity, the importance of which should not be underestimated in medieval civil and ecclesiastical society, Francis and Clare were different in terms of how they expressed their religious convictions (Francis in itinerant mendicancy; Clare in cloistered community) and how long they lived (Francis died in 1226; Clare died almost thirty years later in

1253). Yet they shared in common a similar desire and love, which was not for each other (despite what some misguided romantic depictions to the contrary suggest) but for Jesus Christ and the gospel life. What Clare was drawn to in Francis's preaching was not a charismatic older man (Francis was about twelve years older) but the God about whom he preached.

Clare was fond of describing herself as a *plantacula* ('a little plant') of Francis of Assisi. Over the centuries, this self-reference has been misunderstood as a sign of subjugation and diminution. However, as the Franciscan scholar Bill Short explains:

> In context, however, Clare's name for herself indicates something different: she is separate but connected, rooted in the same soil of the Gospel, sharing with Francis a 'form of life' she received from him as a gift from God. But the way in which she expresses her growing, intimate knowledge of 'following the footsteps of our Lord Jesus Christ' is uniquely her own. What unites Clare and Francis is not an identical experience of Christ, but different experiences of the same Christ.[2]

To understand the Franciscan movement, and more so anything classified as Franciscan prayer, one must have an appreciation for Clare's place alongside Francis as a true co-founder and long-influential shaper of the tradition. According to an early source's account of Clare's death on 11 August 1253, among those gathered at Clare's bedside are Leo, Rufino and Angelo, three of the first followers of Francis. According to the early texts of the tradition, after Francis's death the only time these three central figures are said to have been in the same place at the same time was when Clare embraced 'Sister Bodily Death'. As Bill Short keenly observes, this scene is important – and probably historically accurate given that all three were still alive at the time – because of what is symbolized:

> Clare at the center of the early companions, at the core of the tradition as it is being handed over to the next generation. For this reason, some authors today are beginning to speak of a

'Franciscan-Clarian' tradition. More than a disciple, Clare is also a creative architect of the tradition she lived.[3]

In what ways might we locate the marks of Clare's 'creative architecture' of prayer within the tradition? Though there are surely many other characteristics of Clare's contributions to prayer in the Franciscan tradition and Franciscan spirituality more broadly, for the sake of brevity I suggest that three of the essential Clarian insights are poverty, contemplation and the cross of Christ.

The importance of poverty

Like Francis, Clare had a deeply incarnational spiritual outlook. As Franciscan theologian Ilia Delio has noted, Clare 'viewed the Incarnation as a coincidence of opposites, a mystery of poverty and riches. The one who is rich in mercy and love bends low in the Incarnation to embrace us in love, and it is in accepting this gift of the poor One that we become rich in God.'[4] This incarnational theological outlook grounds Clare's understanding of evangelical poverty, contextualizing the experience of self-offering (*kenosis*) as a means towards an end rather than merely an ascetical end in itself. This end is the deepening of relationship with God as well as increased solidarity with the abject poor and marginalized of society. On this latter point, it is noteworthy that Clare's religious community at the church of San Damiano was also the site of a medieval leper hospice, which was dedicated to caring for these socially and ecclesially disenfranchised people.

This historical fact offers us some additional insight into Clare's own understanding and experience of prayer. Like Francis, Clare was drawn to a life of penance. Simply put, to commit to a 'life of penance' at this time in Christian history meant that one would voluntarily embrace changes in the manner of living that distinguished oneself from the way one previously lived. What motivated that change was one's Christian faith and, for Francis and Clare, the model for the new way of life was the gospel of Jesus Christ. As

Franciscan historian Marco Bartoli observes, '"to do penance" then, was the expression used by all Christians including lay people who wanted to take the Gospel seriously'.[5] From the Franciscan perspective, one could not seriously live the gospel without attending to those who were most disenfranchised and suffering in society. However, unlike Francis and his brother friars whose form of life was expressly itinerant, Clare's particular vision for Franciscan life was much more in line with traditional cloistered communities of women religious at the time. Nevertheless, even Clare and her sisters, who had freely embraced a life of monastic enclosure, continued to perform works of charity informed by their commitment to the *vita evangelica* – the gospel life.

The most spiritually rich and theologically insightful writings we have from Clare are in the form of four short letters written to Agnes of Prague (1205–1282). Agnes was the daughter of King Premsyl Ottokar I of Bohemia and, along with seven other noble women, left behind the status, comfort and security of royalty to enter the newly founded 'Order of Saint Damien' (modelled after Clare's Assisi community at the chapel of San Damiano) in 1234. Though Clare and Agnes never met in person, their brief correspondences over the span of twenty years convey an intimacy and depth in light of their shared admiration of Christ and the life of evangelical poverty, which also evokes what Clare and Francis similarly shared in common. In Clare's 'First Letter to Agnes of Prague', we read:

O blessed poverty, who bestows eternal riches on those who love and embrace her! O holy poverty, God promises the kingdom of heaven and, beyond any doubt, reveals eternal glory and blessed life to those who have and desire her! O God-centered poverty, whom the Lord Jesus Christ Who ruled and still rules heaven and earth, Who spoke and things were made, came down to embrace before all else . . . If so great and good a Lord, then, on coming into the Virgin's womb, wanted to appear despised, needy, and poor in this world, so that people who were very poor and needy, suffering excessive hunger of heavenly nourishment, may become rich in Him by possessing the kingdom of heaven, be very joyful and glad, filled with a remarkable happiness and a spiritual joy![6]

Here and elsewhere in the correspondence, Clare encourages Agnes and her religious sisters continually to focus on the evangelical poverty modelled by Christ in the incarnation. As Ilia Delio notes, 'From the beginning of Clare's letter to Agnes, it is clear that poverty is the key to one's relationship with God. Like Francis, Clare viewed divine revelation as the movement of God to poverty shown in the life of Jesus Christ.'[7] The model for Christian living is the poor God who emptied Godself to become like us in order to enter more deeply into relationship with all people.

Throughout her letters, Clare draws upon royal imagery familiar to Agnes and others of noble standing to illustrate the 'spiritual benefits' of embracing a spirituality and praxis of evangelical poverty: precious stones, priceless pearls, sparkling gems and a golden crown of holiness.[8] Additionally, Clare does not shy away from spousal metaphors, suggesting by way of continuing encouragement in her 'Second Letter to Agnes of Prague', that, 'as someone zealous for the holiest poverty, in a spirit of great humility and the most ardent love, you have held fast to the footprints of Him to whom you merited to be joined in marriage'.[9] Amid this encouragement for fidelity to the call of evangelical poverty in following Christ, Clare offers an original prayer of blessing and exhortation to Agnes, which has become itself a classic of the Franciscan tradition.

What you hold, may you hold,
What you do, may you do and not stop.
But with swift pace, light step, unswerving feet,
so that even your steps stir up no dust,
may you go forward securely, joyfully and swiftly,
on the path of prudent happiness,
believing nothing, agreeing with nothing
that would dissuade you from this commitment

or would place a stumbling block for you on the
    way,
so that nothing prevents you from offering
your vows to the most high in the perfection
to which the spirit of the Lord has called you.[10]

As Timothy Johnson has noted, the spousal imagery Clare uses to talk about Agnes's relation to Christ combines both the royal metaphors with the centrality of evangelical poverty. According to Clare's telling:

> Agnes's spouse is like no other spouse. He is the most royal and noble of grooms, a spouse whose beauty far surpasses all others. Paradoxically, he is also the poorest of the poor, the lowest and most despicable of all men. Agnes has chosen as a spouse the poor, Crucified Christ, whom others rejected, despised, scourged and killed.[11]

Through the personal relationship with Christ, one is able then to embrace a concrete model of evangelical poverty, which, as Delio explains, helps create a space within one's heart to receive what we see in the divine and embrace that which is a personal, relational, loving God.[12]

Visualization and relational imagery play a key role in Clare's style of prayer. While reflecting on the gospel life, encouraging Agnes (and others) in the continual pursuit of evangelical perfection, and relating to Christ as spouse and divine poverty personified, Clare draws on creative descriptors, personal experience and rich illustrations to develop a pattern of mental prayer. This is seen most fully in what we might understand as her instructions to Agnes on contemplation.

The way of contemplation

Although we have relatively few of Clare's writings compared to the collection that has been passed down from Francis, these texts nonetheless reveal to us profound insights into Clare's under-standing and practice of prayer. As with Francis, Clare was deeply drawn to the person of Jesus Christ, and this fascination with Christ 'expresses itself in unceasing prayer'.[13] As we have already seen, Clare's advice to Agnes about persistence in maintaining one's commitment to evangelical poverty is deeply christological, drawing on the incarnate Word as both model for living and source of the call. This incarnational vision carries over into Clare's approach to prayer within the cloistered expression of the Franciscan charism of which she is the undisputed founder. The spousal language sets the context for Clare's instruction on contemplation. Clare writes: 'But as a poor virgin embrace the poor Christ. Look upon Him Who became contemptible for you, and follow Him, making yourself contemptible in this world for Him. Most noble Queen, *gaze, consider, contemplate desiring to imitate your Spouse*.'[14] What Clare lays out is a fourfold process: *intuere* (gaze, focus), *considera* (consider), *contemplare* (contemplate), and *desiderans imitari* (desire to imitate). This pattern is repeated again nearly two decades later in her last letter to Agnes, written shortly before Clare's death. Clare expands on the fourfold formula, now drawing also on the metaphor of the mirror that she writes about in her interim third letter to Agnes.

> Gaze upon that mirror each day, O Queen and Spouse of Jesus Christ, and continually study your face in it, that you may adorn yourself completely, within and without, covered and arrayed in needlework and similarly adorned with the flowers and garments of all the virtues, as is becoming, the daughter and dearest bride of the Most High King. Indeed, in that mirror, blessed poverty, holy humility, and inexpressible charity shine forth as, with the grace of God, you will be able to contemplate them throughout the entire mirror.[15]

As Franciscan scholar Regis Armstrong has commented: 'This for-mula, paradoxically profound in its simplicity, reflects the insights of a woman eager to awaken affection in others for the God of her heart.'[16] Prayer for Clare is the experience of being in love with the God who is Love (1 John 4.8). This loving relationship, though certainly a unique experience for each individual loved into existence by God, nevertheless shares something in common, which is why Clare is comfortable offering a deliberate approach to contemplation to be handed on to others – something that Francis never attempted.

In reflecting on the relationship between evangelical poverty and Clare's way of contemplation, Delio notes that these two elements of Clare's vision of prayer are 'fundamental to Clare's spiritual path'.[17] Because poverty modelled after the example of Christ's own self-emptying example is always understood in the Franciscan tradition as a means towards the greater end of authentic relationship and recognition of our inherent interdependence, it creates something of a path towards or space for the contemplative life. Delio explains:

> Poverty opens the window of the human heart to the love of the Holy Spirit, and it is this love which unveils the beauty of the divine image within the human person. By gazing upon the crucified Christ, one is led not only to the poverty of being human but one is able to recognize the truth of one's being, one's smallness in relation to God's infinite greatness and love. Because poverty provides the space within the human heart for the indwelling of God, it is the condition for openness and receptivity to God, the starting point of our journey into God. As Clare will expound in her letters to Agnes, poverty is the foundation for contemplation and union with God because poverty creates a space within so that God may be born anew.[18]

Contemplation for Clare is never a purely intellectual exercise, but always a deliberate act of the will motivated by love: love of Christ, love of Christ's poverty, love of those that Christ loved. Just as prayer was, for Francis, always about relationship, so too was this the case with Clare's outlook on contemplation. As Delio explains elsewhere: 'Contemplation for Clare begins by *falling in love*. It is being grasped by the power of God's love in the crucified Christ and giving ourselves over to that love.'[19] This act of surrender to the one with whom we are in love is a form of poverty, which is always modelled on the empowering and generative love of Christ.

Much of the contemplative tradition of the Christian Church has focused on the *apophatic*, according to which the dissimilarity between God and creatures leads the contemplative to negate descriptors and metaphors of the divine in an effort to be entirely open and receptive to God. And yet, within the Franciscan tradition exemplified here in Clare's pattern of prayer, contemplation takes on a decidedly *kataphatic* dimension, according to which the contemplative recognizes that: 'there is a discernible similarity between creatures and the Creator. Consequently, it is possible to know and assent to divine realities because creatures are analogically related to the Creator.'[20] Clare's incarnational world view placed God's embrace of the material world generally and the human person specifically at the centre of her experience of and relationship to the divine. As a result, God is not some unknowable 'Other' far away from creation, but an immanent Creator who draws near to creation in love.

Clare's use of striking visual and humanly relational images in discussing prayer with Agnes should be seen to reflect this incarnational primacy in contemplation, which not coincidentally aligns well with the centrality of evangelical poverty exhibited by a God who surrenders even divinity to draw as close as possible in relationship to creation. Johnson has observed:

> Given Clare's decidedly kataphatic spirituality, it is not by chance that she turns frequently to visual language in religious discourse, as opposed to aural language, because it is more apt to convey the sense of immanency proper to the kataphatic contemplative experience.[21]

For instance, instead of 'hearing God's call', which especially in our age with the advent of telephone and digital communications can come from any location and time, the proximity necessary for visual recognition and union presupposes a profound sense of immanence. This closeness to the divine is expressed in Clare's turn towards visual language and, as Johnson notes: 'Her preference for visual language underlines her conviction that Christ will be continually and intimately present to Agnes if she envisions him daily as spouse and mirror.'[22]

It is in the fourth and last letter to Agnes that Clare reveals her own experience of mystical encounter with Christ through this fourfold path of contemplation. She explains that it is in praying before and opening herself to Christ on the cross that she first received the invitation to follow Christ more deeply in evangelical poverty and gospel living. It is perhaps no mere coincidence that Clare spent forty years of her life living with her sisters at the church of San Damiano and in the regular presence of the now-famous crucifix that spoke to Francis, exhorting him to 'rebuild the church'.[23] It is in this first-person recounting of her prayer life so far that Clare's emphasis on spousal metaphor and visual imagery come together in a way deeply evocative of the book of the Song of Songs in the Old Testament. She describes her experience of prayer and relationship to Christ as an encounter with the God who pursues her, which Clare relates to Agnes by way of encouraging her fellow cloistered sister to seek similar union with God. Finally, Clare encourages Agnes to 'rest' in this contemplation.[24] Clare remarks in her closing lines that one's own words begin to appear inadequate in expressing what one experiences so viscerally and proximately. Despite her otherwise kataphatic methodology of approach in contemplation, there remains a notable apophatic conclusion when left to convey the experience of divine embrace.

Among Clare's many contributions to the Franciscan tradition of prayer, too many to adequately present in this little book, we can include her poetic description and kataphatic instruction, both of which are lacking to some degree in Francis's own writings. Clare, inspired as she was by Francis's kindred desire for union with God, develops the gospel exhortation to embrace Christlike poverty into a spirituality of encounter with the living God who indeed empties the divine self to draw near to humanity in the paradoxical movement of kenosis. Her use of spousal metaphor and visual imagery further concretizes the pattern and experience of contemplation as she lived it, offering Agnes and us a simple yet profound guide to respond in love to God's invitation to enter more deeply into relationship. In other words, Clare outlines a path to develop further a journey of prayer and one that leads us to the cross of Christ.

The centrality of the cross

In addition to the love of evangelical poverty and the pattern of contemplation Clare lays out in her letters to Agnes of Prague, the centrality of the cross of Christ plays a notable role in her life of prayer. As noted earlier, Clare is a concrete thinker who provides rich visual illustrations to express the intimate dynamics of divine relationship that characterize prayer. In addition to the spousal imagery she regularly invokes in her spiritual direction to Agnes, she also returns again and again to the image of the crucified Christ. Just as Clare was fascinated with the powerful reality of God's incarnation, that self-emptying embrace of holy poverty for the sake of our salvation, so too she was captivated with the cross of Christ, like Francis before her. But, as Delio notes:

> The idea of contemplation as an indwelling in the mystery of the Crucified is unique to Clare. Contemplation begins with the gaze on Christ crucified and is the penetrating gaze that accepts the disclosure of God in the fragile human flesh of the other, that is, the crucified Christ.[25]

While Francis certainly focused his preaching, admonitions and attention on the cross of Christ, it is Clare who more directly asserts 'the cross is where we come to know God and ourselves in God'.[26]

In her 'Third Letter to Agnes of Prague', Clare poetically weaves together her rich spousal imagery with an invitation to enter more deeply into the mystery of the cross as the source of insight, wisdom and, ultimately, divine union:

And, to use the words of the Apostle [Paul] himself in their proper sense, I judge you to be a co-worker of God Himself and a support for the weak members of His ineffable Body. Who is there, then, who would not encourage me to rejoice over such marvelous joys? Therefore, dearly beloved, may you too always rejoice in the Lord. And may neither bitterness nor a cloud overwhelm you, O dearly beloved Lady in Christ, joy of the angels and crown of your sisters!

Place your mind before the mirror of eternity!
Place your soul in the brilliance of glory!
Place your heart in the figure of the divine sub-
    stance
and, through contemplation,
transform your entire being into the image
of the Godhead Itself,
so that you too may feel what friends feel
in tasting the hidden sweetness
that, from the beginning,
God Himself has reserved for His lovers.[27]

Clare invites us through her own example to be attentive to the cross and to see in it not just a symbol of what has once occurred to Jesus of Nazareth, but to allow the cross to become 'the mirror of eternity', in and through which we are able to explore the depths of ourselves and God.[28] Delio summarizes how Clare understands this dimension of contemplative prayer:

If contemplation is a penetrating truth of reality, it must first lead one to the truth of one's self in God. The cross, therefore, indicates to us the true image of ourselves, and the image we need to gaze upon within ourselves – our own poverty, humility, and suffering. To place oneself in the mirror of the cross is to expose oneself to the joys and sorrows of being human, the joy of God's all-embracing love and the sorrow of seeing the Spouse 'despised, struck, and scourged.'[29]

Clare invites Agnes and, by extension, each of us to meditate on the meaning of the cross in order to reflect more profoundly on the truth revealed about God and ourselves.

Clare's understanding of prayer is much like her understanding of evangelical poverty: it is not an end in itself. While union with the divine is made possible through a life of penance marked by an embrace of poverty and a commitment to contemplation, Clare sees the ultimate goal of gazing on the mirror of the cross as a means towards transformation of the individual. In other words, ongoing conversion is the aim of prayer for Clare; if we take our prayer journeys seriously then we should strive to imitate Christ rather than merely adore or admire Christ from a distance. This is partly the power behind her mirror metaphor, recognizing that contemplation of the cross should invite us into a place of profound introspection in which we consider how we ought to change our ways in order to conform ourselves more fully to the example of Jesus Christ. As Delio explains: 'Just as a mirror, empty in itself, reflects back what is given to it, so, too, the soul purified and illumined reflects the presence of God.'[30] As we progress in our journey of faith and prayer, what is reflected to us in the mirror of the cross ought to increasingly, if at times slowly, becomes more and more aligned with what we can recognize as truly Christian after the pattern of the poor, crucified Christ. Because, after all, that is what the entire Franciscan movement is about: living the gospel and following in the footprints of our Lord Jesus Christ.

Questions for reflection or discussion

1 Clare of Assisi was not merely the 'first woman to follow Francis', but also someone whose own distinctive spiritual contributions helped shape and guide the early Franciscan movement. In what ways do Clare's contributions affirm or challenge your own understanding of the Franciscan tradition?

2 How do you understand evangelical poverty? In what ways might Clare's commitment to evangelical poverty in the spiritual life shape your understanding and experience of prayer?

3 For many people, the crucifixion is seen as an impediment to one's prayer journey, yet Clare makes the cross a central part of her spirituality. What are some of the ways you might follow Clare's lead and incorporate the cross into your prayer journey? What is it that you see when you 'gaze upon the mirror of eternity' that is the cross?

3

Bonaventure: Prophecy and everyday mysticism

Unsurprisingly, many of the central themes in the approaches to prayer presented by Francis and Clare of Assisi appear as guiding principles in St Bonaventure's (*c.* 1217–1274) own writings. The Christ-centred focus, the importance of evangelical poverty, the significance of contemplation and the commitment to embracing a lifelong experience of continuing conversion shape Bonaventure's own contributions to Franciscan prayer. Yet, like his predecessors, Bonaventure also adds his own distinctive elements and broadens the spiritual landscape of resources available in the way of the Franciscans.

Bonaventure is perhaps one of the best known Franciscan figures of the thirteenth century after Francis and Clare of Assisi and Anthony of Padua. He was a learned man and a gifted scholar whose contributions to medieval theology far exceed the ability we have in this chapter to explore. In addition to holding an important professorship at the University of Paris for a time, Bonaventure was elected Minister General (that is, the successor of Francis who oversees the entire Franciscan order) during a particularly tumultuous time in the community's history. He is credited with holding the Franciscan movement together amid disputation and division. His theological genius and leadership prowess caught the eye of church leaders in Rome and he was later made bishop of Albano and then named a cardinal by Pope Gregory X in 1273. He died on 15 July 1274 during the Second Council of Lyons, for which Bonaventure was an organizer appointed by the pope. He was canonized on 14 April 1482 and declared a Doctor of the Church on 14 March 1588 (his title: *Doctor Seraphicus*).

Bonaventure is typically remembered for either his leadership skills or his academic acumen, but is not typically drawn upon as an exemplar or guide in the life of prayer outside of those within the Franciscan family who are familiar with his spiritual writings, including his best-known treatises, *The Soul's Journey into God, The Tree of Life* and *The Major Life of St Francis.*[1] And yet, even in his more 'academic' theological works, including lengthy treatises on Scripture and his expansive commentary on the *Sentences* of Peter Lombard, Bonaventure held prayer to be an essential component of ordinary life. Unlike the contemporary or at least commonly perceived bias against conflating 'popular' or 'spiritual' writing with so-called rigorous scholarly research, Bonaventure's approach was one that married these ostensibly distinct worlds, claiming in fact that they were inseparable. As scholars Charles Carpenter and Gregory LaNave have rightly claimed, academic study was never an end in itself for Bonaventure, but always a means toward holiness, which is the path set before all Christians.[2] Whereas practitioners of Christian prayer today may wish to distance themselves from the 'book learning' of higher studies, Bonaventure at first encouraged his university students and then the friars under his leadership to integrate the two dimensions of their intellectual and spiritual lives. When the Franciscan order struggled with tensions and challenges during the time of his leadership of the community, 'Bonaventure insists that the first step in reform is the renewal of the practice and pursuit of prayer and devotion.'[3]

Bonaventure's own approach to prayer was, as the late Franciscan scholar Zachary Hayes explains, 'a systematic vision deeply rooted in the spiritual experience of St. Francis'.[4] Like the many other women and men who followed Francis of Assisi, Bonaventure's starting point was the lived experience of the saint and founder of this peculiar penitential movement to which he belonged. Hayes notes that Bonaventure 'developed key insights of St. Francis's spirituality into theological and metaphysical doctrines that greatly enrich the Christian tradition of theology'.[5] As Franciscan theologian Richard Martignetti explains: 'Bonaventure's call to prayer is born of his firm belief that we human beings are in complete need of God and complete need of prayer, which is our lifeline to God.'[6] Prayer is the lifeblood of one's faith journey, which not only anchors us in our Christian belief but also fuels and animates our living the gospel in the times and places we find ourselves.

Like Francis and Clare before him, Bonaventure held a deeply incarnational view of prayer, placing Christ both at the centre of the cosmos writ large and within each human heart. With Christ at the centre of all existence, Bonaventure's vision of God was one of a deeply humble and relational Creator who draws near to creation and discloses the divine self completely through the incarnate Word. His understanding of prayer was significantly shaped by this incarnational outlook, such that, as Ilia Delio explains:

> In Bonaventure's view, contemplation cannot be exclusively confined to the soul since the soul itself cannot exist apart from the body. Rather, the Word of God entered into union with the flesh to ennoble our nature by creating the object of contemplation necessary for the beatification of our nature. This object of contemplation for Bonaventure was not the transcendent unknowable God (as it was for the Greeks) but Christ, God and man.[7]

Prayer was not something divorced from the reality of the world, from our corporeal existence, or from the quotidian moments of the ordinary. Instead, precisely because of the God who is revealed as God-for-us through the incarnation, the object of our prayer is the incarnate Word whose own experience of embodiment glorifies the ordinary and the everyday. Mystical experience for Bonaventure was not extra-worldly but intra-worldly and a potential experience for all.

Although there are many paths we could pursue in gaining a deep appreciation for Bonaventure's approach to and theology of prayer, I want to propose that we look at three of the key themes in his way of prayer: imagination, prophecy and contemplation. Each of these elements reflects the continuity of the Franciscan way of

prayer received by Bonaventure while each also reflects the distinctive contributions he made to the tradition.

The necessity of imagination

Imagination is one of those human faculties that we both take for
granted and also, when pressed with providing a cogent definition,
struggle to describe. Some might characterize the imagination as a
flight of fancy, a form of escapism that distracts an individual from
'reality' and the important work of navigating everyday experiences. Others might describe imagination as the condition of the
possibility for creative expression, a way of considering alternative
outcomes or consequences yet to be realized. However one might
understand the term, I find myself agreeing with theologian Sally
Ann McReynolds, who boldly states, 'Imagination is fundamental
to all human activity'. She adds: 'Without imagination that remem-
bers the past, projects possibilities for the future, and shapes human
desire, there can be no action. As the creative, critical, and integra-
tive process central to human becoming, imagination is integral to
the discipline of spirituality.'[8]

While we may not regularly pay much heed to our capacity for
imagination, often thinking of it as something reserved for children, it is in fact an absolutely necessary part of our functioning
in the world. Imagination is the precursor to empathy, a required
tool for future planning and the foundational mechanism for
making ethical choices, since such discernment requires consideration of multiple possibilities and their potential consequences.
Therefore, the use of imagination in prayer would seem to be
something of a foregone conclusion. And yet the operative imagination is often relegated to the background of many discussions
about prayer, necessarily functioning, but doing so largely out of
sight and mind.

In recent centuries, a renewed emphasis on the importance of the
imagination in prayer has gained prominence. This is in large part
due to the successful efforts of the Jesuits and their promotion of
Ignatius Loyola's Spiritual Exercises.[9] What has come to be known

as 'Ignatian spirituality' has included, among its key principles, an emphasis on 'imaginative contemplation'. The aim is to select a story from the Gospels and then place yourself in the scene, imagining that you are there beside the Sea of Galilee with Jesus, feeling the sea breeze and heat from the sun, straining to hear Jesus' preaching to the crowds, touching the dusty earth, considering what feelings the encounter elicits and allowing the Holy Spirit to guide your prayerful encounter with Christ across time and space. It is a beautiful spiritual practice and one that every Christian ought to consider exploring in their prayer journeys. But Ignatius (d. 1556), for all his tremendous contributions to the Christian spiritual tradition and the formation of religious life and ministry, was not the first major Christian figure to develop this explicit engagement with the faculty of the imagination in prayer. What would become identified with the Ignatian tradition in recent years was first developed by the Franciscans.[10]

Around the year 1260, Bonaventure wrote a short spiritual treatise titled the *Lignum vitae*, or *The Tree of Life* in English.[11] Using the image of a tree with twelve branches, each of which bears a 'spiritual fruit' composed of four parts (each part a scene from the New Testament life of Christ), Bonaventure presents forty-eight short vignettes with simple titles like 'Jesus Shown to the Magi' and 'Jesus Denied by His Own'. Central to each vignette are the rich descriptions Bonaventure offers, followed by his direct invitation to the reader to engage the imagination in placing him- or herself in the scene described, considering what it would have been like to be one of the characters in the biblical story, to meditate as an onlooker, or to envisage what the experience must have been like for Jesus at that particular moment. Bonaventure himself explains his intention in the prologue of the text: 'I have used simple, familiar and unsophisticated terms to avoid idle curiosity, to cultivate devotion and to foster the piety of faith.' He adds:

> Since imagination aids understanding, I have arranged in the
> form of an imaginary tree the few items I have collected from

among many, and have ordered and disposed them in such a way that in the first or lower branches the Savior's origin and life are described; in the middle, his passion; and in the top, his glorification.[12]

Throughout *The Tree of Life*, Bonaventure traces the public life of Jesus, inviting us along the way to pause and dwell in the moment presented. He regularly directs the reader's imagination with guiding meditative instructions, such as 'do not now turn away', 'receive the infant in your arms', 'become a companion', 'attend now' and 'breathe in peace now', among many others. One particularly moving scene takes place early in *The Tree of Life* as Bonaventure sets the scene for the birth of Jesus. Drawing on details from the Gospels, Bonaventure reflects:

Although he was great and rich, he became small and poor for us. He chose to be born away from home in a stable, to be wrapped in swaddling clothes, to be nourished by virginal milk and to lie in a manger between an ox and an ass.[13]

Then, focusing on the fragility of the newborn Jesus, Bonaventure turns to the reader to invite us to place ourselves in the scene.

Now, then, my soul, embrace that divine manger; press your lips upon and kiss the boy's feet. Then in your mind keep the shepherd's watch, marvel at the assembling host of angels, join in the heavenly melody, singing with your voice and heart: Glory to God in the highest and on earth peace to men of good will.[14]

The tenderness of the instruction and the attention to the smallest details of human affection – 'kiss the boy's feet' – reflect the instinctual response that any parent or grandparent knows when embracing a newborn child. Yes, the baby Jesus is literally adorable, but what is not lost in Bonaventure's reflection is the actual vulnerability and dependence of Emmanuel, God with us. It is the humanity of Christ, the solidarity that God has with us by virtue of having freely chosen to become *one of us*, that Bonaventure wishes to emphasize and he leads us to this profound theological insight and spiritual truth through our imagination.

Around the same time that Bonaventure composed *The Tree of Life*, he was also inspired to write a short series of poetic meditations on the infancy of Jesus, titled *The Five Feasts of the Child Jesus*.[15] What is distinctive about these moving and simple reflections is the way Bonaventure engages the imagination in order to encourage readers to 'spiritually conceive the holy Word of God and only-begotten Son of the Father, give birth to him, name him, seek and adore him with the Magi, and finally, according to the law of Moses, joyfully present him in the Temple to God the Father'.[16] Here, the imagination is used in prayer not only to enter into the scenes of the young Jesus Christ as a mere observer but also to reflect on how we can be like his mother in the world today and within the circumstances of our own time. This is framed as a journey of the soul, spiritually travelling the path of Mary, conscious of the fact we are also carrying the Word of God within us, even if not as the literal pre-born Jesus. This metaphor is used to guide the imagination of the reader to think concretely about how prayer is actualized in the world through our words and deeds: just as Mary gave birth to Jesus physically, so too we are to bring Christ to birth in the world spiritually.

Following a scene in *The Tree of Life* describing Peter's denial of Jesus after his capture on the night before he died (Matthew 26.69–75; Mark 14.66–72; Luke 22.56–62; John 18.12–27), Bonaventure offers a distinctively lengthy reflection directed at the reader. This instruction is styled as an examination of conscience, which invites the reader to ponder the ways she or he has likewise betrayed Christ in their own context.

O whoever you are, who at the word of an insistent servant, that is your flesh, by will or act have shamelessly denied Christ, who suffered for you, remember the passion of your beloved Master and go out with Peter to weep most bitterly over yourself. When the one who looked upon the weeping Peter looks upon you, you will be inebriated with the wormwood of twofold bitterness: remorse for yourself and compassion for Christ, so that having atoned with Peter for the guilt of your crime, with Peter you will be filled with the spirit of holiness.[17]

Within this short passage, Bonaventure is able to draw from the scriptural episode of Peter's denial and subsequent shame an analogy for our regular experiences of denying Christ implicitly in word and deed. Still, this invitation to reflect on our own sinful acts does not end solely in condemnation and regret, but instead Bonaventure leads us to a place of repentance and hope of sanctity.

At the heart of Bonaventure's use of the imagination in prayer is the centrality of Scripture, which is seen as the guiding principle and focal point of *The Tree of Life*. Shortly before composing that text, Bonaventure wrote a treatise known as *De Triplici Via* or *The Threefold Way*, which offers us an important insight regarding the imagination and the word of God.[18] Imagination is the faculty most suited to help the believer move from a mere literal reading of Scripture into the threefold 'spiritual meaning', which was represented by the moral (the ethical interpretation), allegorical (the deeper meaning beneath the surface of the text) and anagogical (the lifting up of one's heart, mind and soul to the divine) approaches to interpretation. Bonaventure explains: 'This threefold meaning corresponds to three acts hierarchically ordered, that is, purgation, illumination, and perfection. Purgation leads to peace, illumination to truth, and perfection to charity.'[19] By entering more and more deeply into the mystery of Scripture, aided by the imagination, one can probe the depths of its meaning that not only guide the believer in prayer closer to God but also inform and strengthen the believer to put that prayer into action according to peace, truth and charity. Although Bonaventure offers a ready-made guide through forty-eight of the major scenes in the evangelical life of Christ in *The Tree of Life*, his intention is purely illustrative, a model for what the Christian can do in the life of prayer when approaching any passage of Scripture.

The call to prophecy

As we have already seen, Scripture is central to Bonaventure's approach to prayer. The imagination aids a believer in entering more fully into the mystery of Scripture and the life of Jesus Christ when meditating on scenes from the Bible. But Bonaventure did not see this as an end in itself. Instead, he understood that prayer ought to lead us to be agents of God's good news in the world. Not surprisingly, Francis was for him the exemplar of this sort of faith-in-action. According to Bonaventure, Francis models for Christians what it means to be filled with the Spirit, becoming a bearer of the word of God and giving that word birth in the world at this time through word and deed (as he described in his *The Five Feasts of the Child Jesus*). Furthermore, in Bonaventure's estimation, Scripture profoundly shaped Francis in his outlook on the world. And it is through reading, praying and reflecting on Scripture that one's imagination is engaged and a Christian becomes a prophet.

Prophecy is often popularly depicted as the ability to forecast future events. Therefore, the assumption goes, one is a prophet if he or she 'saw it coming'. And while there is some validity in defining prophecy in such terms, it is a limited conception of prophecy and an understanding that merits closer scrutiny. Bonaventure's perspective is informed by the centuries of wisdom about and exploration of the subject that forms the Jewish and then Christian faiths. In what emerges from both the Old Testament and ancient philosophical traditions, the theme of Christian prophecy finds its earliest references in both the canonical and extra-canonical texts of the New Testament era. For instance, we read in the New Testament letters of the various charismatic gifts the Holy Spirit bestows upon the community, including the gift of prophecy. The Greek word used – *prophēteia* – has the connotation 'to speak forth' more than it signifies 'foretelling'. In fact, in its earliest Christian manifestation, prophecy had little to do with one's ability to predict the future. Instead, we see the earliest Christian commentators, drawing on the scriptural use of the term in the Old Testament depictions of the Hebrew prophets, describing prophecy as a particular form of expression. Prophecy is distinct from other declarative forms, not necessarily because of some unique format or style, but because of what was the source or grounding of the expression proclaimed. Here, we see that prophecy is intimately tied to one's ability to read, understand and interpret Scripture, which is the revealed word of God. As such, one no longer sees with the eyes of ordinary human perception, but with the spiritual senses as illumined by grace and the word. Early Christian theologians like Origen (d. *c.* 254 CE) and Augustine of Hippo (d. 430) believed that all Christians were would-be prophets. The key was the individual Christian's openness to a life of prayer guided by the Spirit and immersion in the texts of sacred Scripture.

For Bonaventure, the prophet is one who is able to progress in the reading of Scripture to arrive at its spiritual sense and truest meaning. The more one is able to *read* the Book of Scripture, the more one becomes able to *read* the Book of Life and see the fuller meaning of history past, present and, perhaps sometimes, in the future. This is the core of Bonaventure's understanding of prophecy. Like the earliest Christian references and subsequent patristic commentators, prophecy is not so much about foretelling as it is about *seeing the world as it really is.* In other words, we might say that prophecy is about coming to see the world through the 'eyes of God'. Bonaventure, following Augustine, holds that we are most able to do this by becoming people of Scripture, imbued with God's revelation in a way that informs and reshapes our perceptions. Naturally, justice becomes a primary theme that emerges in the reading of the Book of Life when, with the sense and vision of a prophet, one sees the injustice, marginalization and abuse that occurs throughout our world and in our communities. Like the prophets of Scripture, the Christian prophet 'calls it as he or she sees it' or, to use another colloquialism, 'sees it as it really is'.

It is in his *Legenda Maior*, better known as 'The Life of St Francis', that Bonaventure portrays Francis as a great prophet alongside the greatest prophets of the Old Testament: Daniel, Ezekiel, Moses, and Elijah.[20] We see in the title of chapter eleven – 'The Understanding of Scripture and the Spirit of Prophecy' – precisely how

Bonaventure understands the relationship between Scripture and prophecy in the life of Francis.[21] He opens the chapter with a poetic prelude, setting up a narrative in the pages that followed in which he would narrate and then analyse twelve episodes in Francis's life representative of his prophetic abilities.[22] Only two of the twelve episodes demonstrating Francis's prophetic abilities relate in any way to 'foreseeing the future', while the other ten instances relate instead to contemporaneous events wherein Francis 'contuited secrets of the heart' and 'knew events from afar'.[23]

The central theme here is that the call to prophecy is extended to all Christians through baptism, though many ignore the call or refuse the invitation. It is no wonder that nearly all the Hebrew prophets outright reject God's call to live as prophets in the world, whether Amos who desires to return to his farming duties or Jeremiah who leans on his youthfulness and inarticulateness as proposed excuses for avoiding the prophetic vocation. The way one comes to see the world as God sees it is through a life informed by a biblical imagination, shaped by the narrative of God's self-disclosure, love and mercy conveyed through Scripture. This is one of the consequences, we might say, of taking a life of prayer rooted in Scripture seriously. Once we begin seeing the world as it is alongside the vision of the world as God intends it, we can no longer be silent but find ourselves proclaiming difficult truths about such disparities. Such holding of the powerful in society to account necessarily elicits critical and even threatening responses, which is perhaps why so few women and men consciously embrace the call to prophecy and why prayer can be something frequently avoided even by the faithful. As the twentieth-century Trappist monk Thomas Merton wrote:

> Read the prophets in the Old Testament. Their biggest problem was that they were prophets. Jeremiah didn't want to be a prophet. In some sense, we're in the same boat. God lays on us the burden of feeling the contradictions in our world and church and exposing them, insofar as we are honestly able to do that.[24]

By contrast, Francis of Assisi is the exemplary Christian disciple because he does not shy away from the divine call as had so many of the prophets before him. Instead, as Bonaventure describes it, the commitment to a life of penitential prayer rooted in Scripture inevitably leads to prophecy – seeing the world as it really is and decrying its departure from God's intention for shalom, or true peace. The call to prophecy in Bonaventure's understanding of prayer is one more distinctive element in the way of the Franciscans.

Contemplation and everyday mysticism

In the last chapter, we saw how Clare of Assisi contributed to the diverse way of Franciscan prayer through a distinctive pattern or guide to contemplation. Clare's approach was one centred on the fourfold process of gazing, considering, contemplating and, ultimately, striving to imitate Christ. The poverty of Christ in the incarnation and the humility of Christ on the cross serve as the primary focal points of her way of contemplative prayer. In this sense, Clare's approach is rather traditional and not that different from the guided meditation and methods of contemplation found in other religious communities, especially within monastic traditions (though she inarguably adds a Franciscan spin to it). However, Bonaventure's approach is actually more innovative, that is, if we have eyes to see what he's doing in his rather sophisticated theological treatises and spiritual writings.

Like Clare, Bonaventure offers a pattern or structure in what is undoubtedly his most famous text, the *Itinerarium Mentis in Deum*, or 'The Soul's Journey into God' in English.[25] Whereas Clare proposed something of a four-step journey of contemplation, Bonaventure proposes a six-step journey, which was inspired by an experience reflecting on Francis's receiving the stigmata on Mount La Verna, at which time tradition states that Christ appeared to Francis in the form of a six-winged seraph angel. Those six wings become symbolic for Bonaventure, offering six stages of ascent towards union with God.

Like Clare, Bonaventure is attentive to the discipline of contemplation. However, unlike Clare's use of the traditional Latin word *contemplatio* for 'contemplation', Bonaventure uses another word – *speculatio* – which can be a difficult word to translate from the Latin in the *Itinerarium*. Its root is used in various forms throughout the text, which signals Bonaventure's deliberate emphasis on the nuances of its meaning. As Regis Armstrong explains:

> The etymological root of speculum and speculatio is species (sight, appearance), which brings together the object, the mirror (speculum) that reflects the created world in which the beholder lives, and activity of seeing (speculatio) by which the beholder, as a unique piece of that created world, takes it in and understands what it reveals.[26]

Therefore, like Clare, Bonaventure also uses the image of a mirror throughout his reflections on contemplative prayer. However, while Clare focuses on the cross of Christ as the mirror into which one gazes, contemplates and considers in order to then imitate the poor, crucified Christ, Bonaventure applies the mirror imagery throughout the entirety of creation, describing each aspect of creation as a vestige (*vestigium*) of the Creator. Each aspect of creation, sentient or otherwise, bears an 'imprint' (*vestigium*) of God, which serves as a mirror of the Trinity reflecting the triune God back to those who have trained their eyes to see.

While related in some ways to Clare's particular approach to contemplation, Bonaventure's distinctive contribution is more focused outwards, concerned as he is not just with setting aside time in the chapel to meditate on the cross interiorly but also with seeing and interpreting the world around us exteriorly. In this way, Bonaventure weds the mirror imagery of Clare's contemplative prayer with Francis's journey to become 'a living prayer'. The framework of the *Intinerarium* is a journey of ascent that involves a twofold process of moving 'through' and 'in' each of three levels (for a total of six steps). Before commencing the prayer journey towards greater communion with God, Bonaventure opens his text with a prayerful invocation, calling the reader to be mindful of the prayerful spirit needed to proceed.

> I call upon the eternal Father through the divine Son, our Lord Jesus Christ, that through the intercession of the most holy virgin Mary, the mother of that same Lord and God, Jesus Christ, and through the intercession of blessed Francis, our leader and father, God might grant enlightenment to the eyes of our mind and guidance to our feet on the path of peace – that peace which surpasses all understanding. This is the peace which our Lord Jesus Christ proclaimed and granted to us. It was this message of peace which our father Francis announced over and over, proclaiming it at the beginning and the end of his sermons.[27]

The images of light, seeing and peace, which Bonaventure highlights, echo throughout the prologue and into the body of the text.

Rather than start at some rarefied or abstract spiritual place, Bonaventure invites the spiritual seeker to begin his or her prayer journey in the 'visible world', recognizing that every aspect of creation around us is a *vestigium* of God – a mirror we may look 'through' and 'in' to reach a deeper understanding of who God is and who we are called to be. The first step focuses on the external world. Bonaventure notes that our own sinfulness, what Augustine called our concupiscence, inhibits our ability to recognize the divine mirror in creation. We are, to use the Augustinian image Bonaventure adopts, 'bent over' ourselves, in a posture that is like navel-gazing. Unable to see straight, our vision is obscured and our recognition of God in creation is prevented. Unsurprisingly, Bonaventure believes that the antidote to such sinfully impaired spiritual vision is reading and praying with sacred Scripture. Through meditating on the word of God, we are able to come back to the sensible reality all around us and of which we are a part in order to see more clearly God reflected in creation.

Bonaventure concludes this step with the instruction: 'Therefore open your eyes, alert your spiritual ears, unlock your lips, and apply your heart so that in all creation you may see, hear, praise, love and adore, magnify and honor your God.'[28]

The second step is coming to a greater awareness of what it is we begin to recognize in the visible world through the first step of the contemplative journey. Bonaventure describes this as moving from seeing God 'through' visible reality to seeing God 'in' visible reality. What he means by this is that the more we attune our spiritual senses to God's presence *in creation*, the more we recognize all of creation's dependence on God, who is always already sustaining us. Bonaventure writes:

> With respect to the mirror of sensible things, it is possible that God might be contemplated not only through them, but also in them in as far as God is present in them by essence, power, and presence . . . Therefore it is a second level of contemplation by which we ought to be led to the contemplation of God in all those creatures that enter into our mind through the bodily senses.[29]

The third and fourth steps shift to focus on the image of God in our minds. The starting point for Bonaventure's approach to contemplation is deeply empirical, rooted in creation and literally *grounded* in the world. This then leads to a twofold stage of critical interiority in which we are invited to reflect on the Trinity and the way in which God is present to us, precisely as dwelling *in us* as divine grace. He writes:

> Flooded with all these intellectual lights, our mind – like a house of God – is inhabited by the divine Wisdom. It is made to be a daughter of God, a spouse and friend. It is made to be a member, a sister, a coheir of Christ the Head. It is made into the temple of the Holy Spirit, grounded in faith, elevated in hope, and dedicated to God through holiness of mind and body. It is the most sincere love of Christ that brings this about,

a love which is poured forth in our hearts through the Holy Spirit who is given to us. And without this Spirit we cannot know the secret things of God.[30]

The process of ascent to God, beginning with the world around us and leading to us reflecting internally on God, continues in a direction that leads us increasingly towards God.

Finally, the last two steps reflect Bonaventure's longstanding commitment to what he calls the anagogical approach to Scripture and prayer, meaning that contemplation ultimately leads us beyond ourselves and the material world to experience God as such, even if we can never fully know or experience the incomprehensible mystery that is the Creator. If one is able to ascend to God through this six-stage process of contemplation (*speculatio*), then what God has in store for us is revealed in that encounter with the divine. Contemplation for him is not merely an intellectual exercise, but one of continuing conversion of death to the old self in order to put on Christ. Ultimately, the journey of prayer is about entering into deeper relationship with the Creator through divine love. Bonaventure writes:

> Now if you ask how all these things are to come about, ask grace, not doctrine; desire, not intellect; the groaning of prayer and not studious reading; the Spouse, not the mater; God, not a human being; darkness, not clarity; not light, but the fire that inflames totally and carries one into God through spiritual fervor and with the most burning affections. It is God alone who is this fire, and God's furnace is in Jerusalem. And it is Christ who starts the fire with the white flame of his most intense passion. Only that person who says: My soul chooses hanging, and my bones death, can truly embrace this fire. Only one who loves this death can see God, for it is absolutely true that no one can see me and live.[31]

The journey of contemplation for Bonaventure is one that begins with the mundane, the everyday experiences and encounters in the world, which seen anew and with a mind and heart oriented towards reflecting on God's presence through and in creation, allows us to draw closer and closer to God.

Bonaventure's way of prayer is an invitation to experience 'everyday mysticism', that training of the spiritual senses to recognize the presence of God always already near to us. Like Augustine before him, Bonaventure believes that God is the one who is closer to us than we are to ourselves, which to those who may refuse to embark on the soul's journey to God seems like a frightening reality, but for those who open themselves up, attune themselves to God's revelation in Scripture and creation, and seek the divine in the ordinariness of their lives and world, it is a sign of assurance and peace.

Questions for reflection or discussion

1 Scripture and imagination are two central elements of prayer for Bonaventure. How do you incorporate Scripture into your prayer journey? What happens when you allow yourself to engage your imagination in prayer?

2 How do you understand prophecy? In what ways do you recognize the call to prophecy in your own life? In what ways do you find yourself resisting that call?

3 What about Bonaventure's approach to contemplation resonates with you? What about it do you find yourself resisting? How can you cultivate a greater sense of 'everyday mysticism' in your prayer journey?

4

Angela of Foligno: Love of Christ, love of the world

On 9 October 2013, during the first year of his pontificate, Pope Francis declared Blessed Angela of Foligno (d. 1309) a saint. Angela was the fourth person canonized by Pope Francis, and undoubtedly a surprise to many people. Whereas many Franciscan saints past and present – Francis, Clare, Anthony of Padua, Bonaventure, Padre Pio, and so on – are what we might call 'household names' because of their popularity and widespread renown, Angela's canonization took many modern people by surprise given her relative anonymity. But just because most Christians did not recognize Angela's name at first glance does not mean that she shouldn't be better known, read and appreciated. Like the other, better-known Franciscans considered so far in this book, Angela is a major contributor to the Franciscan way of prayer. In addition to two lengthy primary texts known as the *Memorial* and the *Instructions*, which together compose her spiritual *Liber,* or 'Book', Angela's own story is a captivating journey of life, loss, conversion and mysticism worthy of consideration in its own right. This is especially true given her status as a medieval laywoman who was neither a cleric nor a woman religious, but a wife and mother.

Born in the small Italian town of Foligno, just a few miles from Assisi, around the year 1248, Angela is believed to have come from a wealthy family and would spend nearly her entire life in that town.[1] Scholars know very little about her life before 1285, when she had a self-described conversion experience. It is generally accepted that she was married when she was about twenty years old, though her husband's identity remains lost to history. From her own accounting in the *Memorial*, we know that Angela had several children and that her immediate household included her mother.[2] All indications show that she lived a comfortable domestic life, which changed significantly when, around 1285, she began experiencing guilt for the manner according to which she had been living. As the late Franciscan historian Paul Lachance summarized: 'Fiery, passionate, impetuous by temperament, Angela seems to have enjoyed the comforts and luxuries of the world before she entered her way of penance.'[3] Angela recounts that she 'wept bitterly' as she reflected on her life to date, and 'the fear of being damned to hell' led her to seek out sacramental confession from the local priest.[4] It was around this point that Angela, inspired by the life and legacy of Francis of Assisi, turned to him in intercessory prayer, asking that he aid her in her new zealotry for a life of penance. Francis appeared to her in a dream, assuring her of his support and encouraging her spiritual journey.

Not long after her profound experience of conversion, Angela sought out the spiritual assistance of a local Franciscan friar known as Brother Arnaldo (also known as 'Brother A' or 'brother scribe' in the *Liber*). Tradition holds that he was a distant relative of Angela's, and that he later served as her spiritual counsellor and scribe, writing down the mystical insights she conveyed into what would become the *Memorial*. For several years, she sought a life of penance while balancing the responsibilities of family life and motherhood within the affluent context of her surroundings. In her writings, she laments the challenge that such circumstances placed on her growing desire to live a penitential life. And then suddenly, around the year 1288, all the members of her immediate family – husband, children, mother – died. While we have virtually no details about the causes of their deaths, we do know that Angela both genuinely mourned their loss while also rejoicing in the newfound freedom she received in then being able to pursue her life of penance unencumbered.[5] Without familial obligations to negotiate, Angela was able to use her social privilege and financial resources to fashion a life of Christian penance that aligned more comfortably with her continuing experience of conversion.

Around 1291, Angela made a pilgrimage to the nearby town of Assisi to visit the new Basilica of St Francis, where she had a powerful spiritual experience. She heard God speak to her directly: 'My daughter, my dear and sweet daughter, my delight, my temple, my beloved daughter, love me, because you are very much loved by me; much more than you could love me.'[6] She then recounts that God said to her:

> I have found a place to rest in you; now you in turn place yourself and find your own rest in me. You prayed to my servant Francis and because my servant Francis loved me very much, I, therefore, did much for him. And if there was any other person who loved me still more, I would do even more for him. And I will do for you what I did for my servant Francis, and more if you love me.[7]

At about the same time, a female spiritual companion named Masazuola, who looked after Angela's practical needs, joined her as Brother Arnaldo continued the work of transcribing her spiritual experiences and mystical visions. Angela kept divesting herself of the family property in order to embrace evangelical poverty in the spirit of Francis and Clare more fully.

From about 1291 until her death in 1309, Angela became renowned in the Umbrian region of Italy as a mystic and spiritual director. Many Franciscan friars and laypeople sought her wisdom and guidance, and her two-part *Liber* – the *Memorial* and the *Instructions* – became a contemporary spiritual classic. Despite lacking a formal theological education, so revered was she for her spiritual insights that she became known as the *magistra theologorum*, that is, 'teacher of theologians'.[8]

Angela's writings offer us a treasure of distinctive resources that highlight her unique contribution to the Franciscan spiritual tradition. In many ways, her *Memorial* and *Instructions* reflect a synthesis of elements we have seen so far in the contributions of Francis, Clare and Bonaventure. Like her Franciscan predecessors, Angela's approach to prayer is deeply christocentric, focuses on evangelical poverty, engages the imagination and offers a clear pattern or process for contemplation. However, Angela's approach to prayer is also notably distinctive in voice, imagery and the number of stages in pursuing the contemplative life. On this latter point, whereas Clare offered Agnes of Prague four stages and Bonaventure uses the six-winged seraph as a template for mystical assent, Angela describes a staggering thirty stages in her *Memorial*. The scope and content of her entire approach to the way of prayer far exceeds the limitations of this chapter, but we can still garner a rich appreciation for her contribution by looking at the way two major spiritual themes are present throughout her writings; namely, her love of Christ and love of the world.

Love of Christ

One of the consistent threads of Franciscan prayer across time and the key contributors we have examined so far is the tradition's profound christocentricity – that is, emphasis on placing Jesus Christ at the centre of one's spiritual journey, Christian outlook and way of prayer. Like Francis, Clare and Bonaventure before her, Angela is drawn to the humility and poverty of God in Christ, especially his experience on the cross. She understood that the cross of Christ was not merely a one-time event on Good Friday, but a theological motif present throughout the life, death and resurrection of the Lord.

> For all his life the suffering God-man knew only one state: that of the cross. His life began on the cross, continued on the cross, and ended on the cross. He was always on the cross of poverty, continual pain, contempt, true obedience, and other harsh deeds of penance.[9]

In true Franciscan form, the suffering of Christ is reflective of the highest poverty embraced by God through the incarnation. Angela explains in the *Instructions*:

We have an example of true poverty in Jesus Christ, God and man. This God and man Jesus Christ raised us up and redeemed us by poverty. His poverty was truly ineffable, for it concealed so much of his total power and nobility.[10]

The poverty of God, the willingness to take on our lowly human state, serves as a constant focal point for Angela. In an early passage in the *Instructions* that deals overtly with prayer, she connects the Franciscan focus on the cross and poverty of Christ with prayer itself. She says: 'And pray in this fashion, namely, always reading the Book of Life, that is, the life of the God-man Jesus Christ, whose life consisted of poverty, pain, contempt and true obedience.'[11]

This notion of the 'Book of Life', which is a recurring theme in Angela's reflections on prayer, offers spiritual seekers an anchor point in their journeys of faith. The life of Christ, the model of being-in-the-world that Jesus of Nazareth presents to us and that is recounted in the Gospels, ought to be the guiding narrative of our own efforts to live in the world. Angela goes so far as to state that: 'Those who possess *the spirit of true prayer* will have the Book of Life, that is, the life of Jesus Christ, God and man, set before them, and everything they could want they will find there.'[12] If prayer is understood as the means to greater communion with God – something Angela asserts when she writes, 'The purpose of prayer is nothing other than to manifest God and self'[13] – then she makes clear that the only way one achieves that mystical union is through Christ.

Whereas she offers guidance to spiritual seekers most directly in the *Instructions*, her *Memorial* recounts her own experiences of prayer and divine union. This part of her *Liber* lends her spiritual direction about prayer a sense of authority grounded in her own encounters with God in Christ. In one passage, Angela recalls an experience of prayer that evokes Clare's own instructions to gaze and contemplate on the cross of Christ in order to imitate him.

Once I was at Vespers and was gazing at the cross. And while I was thus gazing at the cross with the eyes of the body, suddenly my soul was set ablaze with love; and every member of my body felt the greatest joy. I saw and felt that Christ was within me, embracing my soul with the very arm with which he was crucified. This took place right at the moment when I was gazing at the cross or shortly afterward. The joy that I experienced to be with him in this way and the sense of security that he gave to me were far greater than I had ever been accustomed to. Henceforth my soul remained in a state of joy in which it understood what this man, namely Christ, is like in heaven, that is to say, how we will see that through him our flesh is made one with God.[14]

Angela's imagery is so visceral, so embodied and poetic. Clare, for example, drew from the images and contexts of the medieval noble classes to convey the intimacy with Christ that prayer provides. In contrast, Angela's use of the imagination, recollection of mystical visions and seeming fearlessness in starkly describing her encounters with the divine are at once expansive and also deeply personal.

Angela's love of Christ, while always tied to the cross as her primary leitmotif, also drew her more and more deeply into appreciating the Eucharist. In the *Memorial*, she recounts a vision she had while at the celebration of the Mass. Brother A reports:

On another occasion she said she had seen the Christ Child in the host. He appeared to her as someone tall and very lordly, as one holding dominion. He also seemed to hold something in his hand as a sign of his dominion, and he sat on a throne. But I cannot say what he was holding in his hands. I saw this with my bodily eyes, as I did everything I ever saw of the host. When this vision occurred I did not kneel down like the others and I cannot recall whether I ran right up to the altar or whether I was unable to move because I was in such a delightful contemplative state. I know that I was also very upset because the priest put down the host on the altar too quickly. Christ was so beautiful and so magnificently adorned. He looked like a child of twelve. This vision was such a source of joy for me that I do not believe I shall ever lose the joy of it. I was also so sure of it that I do not doubt a single detail of it . . . I simply delighted in seeing that inestimable beauty.[15]

Her love of Christ in the Eucharist repeats throughout the narration of her story and is reflected in her many mystical visions. Elsewhere in the *Memorial*, Angela says, 'And when I receive communion I experience an indescribable feeling of God's presence'. A few lines later, she adds a passing reflection that is reminiscent of Francis's own love of Christ in the Eucharist, particularly as it represents God's humility and love for humanity. Angela explains: 'That communion led my soul to this perception and desire, namely, to want to give itself totally to Christ because it saw that Christ gave himself totally to us.'[16]

Angela's use of metaphor to describe her experiences of prayerful union with God is undoubtedly one of her most distinctive contributions to the Franciscan way of prayer. Towards the end of her *Memorial*, we come across an image that is striking; namely, Angela's description of Christ's cross as her 'bed' upon or within which she rests. It is in many ways an extension of her earlier reflections on the presence of the cross in the life of Christ throughout his earthly pilgrimage, from birth until crucifixion. On one occasion, she recounts to her scribe the manner in which she regularly experienced divine intimacy through prayer and contemplation. Midway through her recollection, she breaks into song, conveying her joy at union with God through a laud.

> It began in this continual fashion on a certain occasion when I was given the assurance that there was no intermediary between God and myself. Since that time there has not been a day or a night in which I did not continually experience this joy of the humanity of Christ. At this moment, my desire is to sing and praise:
>
> I praise you God my beloved;
> I have made your cross my bed.

For a pillow or cushion,
I have found poverty,
and for other parts of the bed,
suffering and contempt to rest on.[17]

Immediately following this reflection, Angela's scribe inserts himself back into the narrative to note that he asked her to explain what exactly she meant by this metaphor in prayer. She responded:

This bed is my bed to rest on because on it Christ was born, lived, and died. Even before man sinned, God the Father loved this bed and its company (poverty, suffering, and contempt) so much that he granted it to his Son. This is why this bed is my bed, namely, the cross where Christ suffered in his body and much more in his soul, and on it I have placed myself and I have found my rest.[18]

Historical theologian Katherine Wrisley Shelby describes Angela's experience of and reflections on Christ as 'performative'.[19] Wrisley Shelby notes:

Angela of Foligno is famous for encountering a Christ who is personally involved with every aspect of her spiritual journey . . . The Christ we encounter in her *Memorial* cannot be bound by theological concepts; rather, he is a living, breathing, loving being with a distinct personality who forms an intimate yet unique relationship with Angela by consistently conversing one on one with her.[20]

This helps us to understand the depth and distinction of Angela's Franciscan spirituality and approach to prayer. She draws from her predecessors in a way that directs her attention to characteristics of the penitential life modelled by Christ, while also engaging the imagination in prayer in such a way as to bring the humanity and cross of Christ to life in a nearly tangible way. Her love of Christ was not simply affection for a theological idea or an evangelical narrative contained in Scripture, but a living, dynamic and active encounter with God. Through this relationship with Christ, Angela was able to recalibrate her own life, choosing as best she could to imitate Christ's manner of being in the world, which led her not only to a deepening love of God but also a love of the world.

Love of the world

Among the manifold approaches to prayer within the Franciscan tradition, one consistent hallmark is the acceptance and embrace of our embodiment and creatureliness. We see this in the importance placed on the incarnation and the attention to the cross along with the suffering implied in the crucifixion, both of which emphasize the humanity of Christ. We also see this in the kataphatic or descriptive language used to express one's relationship with God and God's relationship with the world. Unlike some ancient gnostic and medieval heretical traditions, the Franciscans do not shy away from the world and go to great lengths to affirm the goodness of creation and God's presence in the created world. Angela is no different. As Paul Lachance says regarding Angela's embodied spirituality: 'It is significant to note that it was largely through the body that the intimate and tangible love of Christ crucified communicated itself to Angela.'[21] He adds that, throughout Angela's *Liber*, we encounter numerous instances in which her experiences of prayer are deeply tied to the physical, material, sensorial world. Her experience of spirituality, recognizing the presence of the divine, takes place *within* the context of her ordinary, everyday life.

> She sees with the eyes of the spirit an incredible variety of visions of Christ and a [view] of the world filled to overflowing with the divine presence; hears Christ speaking to her and, in the final stages [of her spiritual journey], saying 'most high words' that cannot be written; smells indescribable sweet odors; feels the warmth of the divine embrace holding her tightly; and on many occasions feels her bones dislocating so

that she can hear them cracking. At one point, Masazuola, her companion, reports seeing Angela's aura, like a multicolored star emanating from her body; at another point, her face radiant and her eyes shining like candles.[22]

Lachance adds, 'in the context of Angela's prayer life, she highly valued bodily forms of prayer, as the first school of spiritual transformation, one never to be abandoned'.[23] Angela's embodied spirituality offers a bridge from her contemplative focus on love of the cross and the poverty of Christ crucified to love of the world in which God became incarnate and of which we are all a part.

This notion of a bridge is even reflected in the *Memorial*, in which Angela offers a meditation on a vision she had of God's love and the recognition of her own struggles to emulate that love in the world. She explains:

> I saw in myself two sides and it was as if these had been separated by a furrow. On one side I saw fullness of love and every good which was from God and not from me. On the other side I saw myself as arid and saw that nothing good originated in me. By this I discovered that it was not I who loved – even though I saw myself as total love – but that which loved in me came from God alone. Afterward God's love and mine converged, which brought about an even greater and more burning love than before. As a result, my desire was to hasten toward that love.[24]

To some modern readers, Angela's rhetoric may seem self-flagellating or unnecessarily critical, but it is rooted in a foundational conviction of Franciscan spirituality; namely, that all good things come from God and return to God. As Francis of Assisi says in his *Admonitions*:

> even if you were more handsome and richer than everyone else, and even if you worked miracles so that you put demons to flight: all these things are contrary to you; nothing belongs

to you; you can boast in none of these things. But we can boast in our weaknesses and in carrying each day the holy cross of our Lord Jesus Christ.[25]

In many ways, Angela offers a more hopeful or optimistic spin on this same insight. While she recognizes the limitation or absence of her love when compared to God's for her, she celebrates the union of divine and human love that spurs her onwards in love of the world. A few paragraphs later in the *Memorial*, she describes the effects such mystical encounters with divine love in prayer provide for her:

When that love leaves me I nonetheless remain so totally contented, so angelic, that I can love reptiles, toads, serpents, and even devils. Whatever I see happening, even mortal sin, does not disturb me; that is, it causes me no displeasure, for I believe that God in his justice permits it. And even if a dog were to devour me, I would not care, and it seems to me that I would not feel the pain or suffer from it.[26]

There are several episodes recounted in the *Memorial* and *Instructions* that reflect precisely this divine bliss that affords Angela the capacity to love others, especially those considered abhorrent because of sin or repugnant because of illness or material poverty, which would not have been possible ordinarily.

One of the most famous episodes in Angela's life appears in the *Memorial* and narrates her experience of ministering to lepers in a local hospital on Maundy Thursday of Holy Week. She opens the story by stating that she was inspired to tell her companion that they should 'go out and find Christ' and that he is most likely to be found at the hospital 'among the poor, the suffering, and the afflicted'. She tells of how she and her companion first distributed some food to the hospitalized and then began washing the ill, which is all the more apropos on the night commemorating Jesus's washing the feet of his disciples at the Last Supper. True to Angela's idiosyncratic form, something unusual transpires in the process.

And after we had distributed all that we had, we washed the feet of the women and the hands of the men, and especially those of one of the lepers which were festering and in advanced stage of decomposition. Then we drank the very water with which we had washed him. And the drink was so sweet that, all the way home, we tasted its sweetness and it was as if we had received Holy Communion. As a small scale of the leper's sores was stuck in my throat, I tried to swallow it. My conscience would not let me spit it out, just as if I had received Holy Communion.[27]

Admittedly, it is a somewhat discomfiting story and probably not a physical spiritual practice that would be advisable on account of health and safety. Nevertheless, there is a lot to unpack here, including Angela's experience of continuing conversion mirroring that of Francis, who himself described encountering lepers as at first 'too bitter' but over time he came, through divine grace, to recognize that 'what had seemed bitter to me was turned into sweetness of soul and body'.[28]

As off-putting as it may be to think about drinking from the wash basin used to clean the wounds of the seriously ill and lepers, the renowned historical theologian Caroline Walker Bynum has noted that 'there were several other Italian saints who ate pus or lice from poor or sick bodies, thus incorporating into themselves the illness and misfortune of others'.[29] Undoubtedly, such practices represent an extreme form of asceticism; nevertheless, they are in keeping with those who embraced the penitential life. Angela's theological reflection on the encounter with the leper and the events that transpired are joined to her eucharistic spirituality. Such practices of love in the world, particularly when expressed towards those who were the least lovable to her, were only made possible because of the communion of love she experienced with Christ. In this way, her actions were understood to be a radical exercise of imitating Christ, who humbled himself to serve the poor and vulnerable in this world.

Another powerful example of Angela's love of the world appears in her *Memorial* and recalls a vision she had of the cosmos.

Afterward [God] added: 'I want to show you something of my power.' And immediately the eyes of my soul were opened, and in a vision I beheld the fullness of God in which I beheld and comprehended the whole of creation, that is, what is on this side and what is beyond the sea, the abyss, the sea itself, and everything else. And in everything that I saw, I could perceive nothing except the presence of the power of God, and a manner totally indescribable. And my soul in an excess of wonder cried out: 'The world is pregnant with God!' Wherefore I understood how small is the whole of creation – that is, what is on this side and what is beyond the sea, the abyss, the sea itself, and everything else – but the power of God fills it to overflowing.[30]

This is one of my favourite passages from Angela's writings. The beauty of the imagery and the creativity in articulating the power of God's immanence in creation is stunning. While Clare and, to a lesser extent, Francis and Bonaventure drew on feminine images to express communion with God, Angela takes it to an inspiring new level in proclaiming: 'The world is pregnant with God!'

All of these insights and expressions of divine union and love of the world flow from a life of prayer and contemplation. Angela continually attributes her worldly mystical encounters and acts of charity as flowing directly from the love of God she encounters in prayer. In her *Instructions,* she explains:

This vision of supreme Being also stirs up in the soul a love corresponding and proportionate to its object, for it teaches us to love everything which receives its existence from the supreme Being . . . When the soul sees the supreme Being stoop down lovingly toward creatures, it does likewise. Thus the supreme Being makes me love those who love him.[31]

Towards the end of the *Instructions,* Angela recounts that this way of prayer is indeed a gradual journey. She says: 'It is in prayer that one finds God. There are three schools of prayer, that is three types of prayer, without which one does not find God. These are bodily, mental, and supernatural.'[32] The bodily is associated with rote prayers (for example, the Our Father or Hail Mary) and physical gestures like the sign of the cross; the mental is about meditating on God at a deeper level; and the supernatural is what results in the mystical visions Angela frequently recounts. These three types follow one after the other, leading the Christian to greater intimacy with God and therefore greater clarity about one's self and the world.

> In these three schools of prayer you come to know who you are and who God is. From the fact that you know, you love. Loving, you desire to possess what you love. And this is the sign of true love: that the one who loves is transformed, not partially but totally into the Beloved.[33]

Questions for reflection or discussion

1 Angela of Foligno has been frequently misunderstood and overlooked throughout much of Christian history. What are the times when you felt misunderstood in your prayer life or experience of God? Have you withheld sharing spiritual experiences for fear of being misunderstood? Are there people you have been quick to dismiss because their experiences of prayer differ from you own?

2 In true Franciscan form, Angela focuses a lot on the humanity of Christ, particularly his suffering on the cross. How do you approach reflecting on the life of Christ in your prayer? What place does the cross have in your spiritual journey?

3 Love of Christ and the visceral experience of God's love lead Angela to love the world and all people, especially the most marginalized and suffering, more deeply. In what ways do you need to work on loving the world and others? How might Angela's approach to and experience of prayer inspire or challenge you in this way?

5

John Duns Scotus: Discovering God and our true self

For many people, to read and study the work of the medieval Franciscan John Duns Scotus (*c.* 1265–1308) can be a burdensome endeavour. Scotus, though he died young in his early forties, left behind a significant body of influential work that is admittedly dense and technical. Yet those who are interested in exploring the Franciscan approach to prayer in its fullest detail may find themselves enduring the difficulties of some of his writing, while others can certainly benefit from his distinctive contributions, even if they understandably want to avoid his arcane style. As a Franciscan friar, Scotus is an inheritor of and a contributor to the rich and dynamic spiritual tradition that began with the example of Francis of Assisi and was developed and expanded by all those we have so far examined in this book. However, as philosopher Mary Beth Ingham reminds us, Scotus is sadly too often seen only as a participant and leader in the Franciscan intellectual tradition, without due regard for his role in the spiritual life of the same community.[1]

Love is the foundational lens through which Scotus views his relationship to God, to others and to creation.[2] But, admittedly, love is an amorphous term. The confusion surrounding its meaning is complicated further by the English language's lack of specificity and our unfortunate tendency to overuse the word. When used in its proper context, love is perhaps one of the most powerful words in the English language. Its authentic use connotes sacrifice, care, concern, selflessness, affection, self-gift, passion, tenderness, consideration, loyalty, respect, attraction, fidelity and other feelings or experiences that transcend language altogether. This powerful word is at the core of Scotus's world view. His entire system evolves from and revolves around love.

In his *Tractatus De Primo Principio* ('Treatise On God as First Principle'), Scotus includes prayers throughout his rigorous philosophical speculation. The prayers themselves reveal a friar-scholar who is as much a man of faith as he is an eminent philosopher. But the inclusion of these invocations also provides us with insight into his understanding of the unity of faith and reason, as well as the necessity of divine assistance in exploring the depths of such profound mysteries. He opens *De Primo Principio* with the following prayer:

O Lord our God, true teacher that you are, when Moses your servant asked you for your name that he might proclaim it to the children of Israel, you, knowing what the mind of mortals could grasp of you, replied: 'I am who am,' thus disclosing your blessed name. *You are truly what it means to be, you are the whole of what it means to exist.* This, if it be possible for me, I should like to know by way of demonstration. Help me then, O Lord, as I investigate how much our natural reason can learn about that true being which you are if we begin with the being which you have predicated of yourself.[3]

As noted, this short passage presents Scotus as someone beyond simply an inquiring mind. He shows himself to be a thinker who is deeply connected to the object of his study and reflection – that is, God – in a personal relationship. He connects his proceeding endeavour with the source of its origin. And he acknowledges that God is the definition of what it means to be and it is only with God's assistance that he might come to understand anything correctly. The late Scotist scholar Allan Wolter, in his commentary on this text, tells us that this prayer, while perhaps seeming extraneous to modern philosophers who would not introduce a scholarly text with such transparent spirituality or prayer, was extracted from the original text and showcased in a condensed form in a collection of ascetical writings that was widely circulated.[4] At some time, the prayers of Scotus were considered to be of value enough to be rewritten.[5]

Scotus's primary aim in his treatise *De Primo Principio* is to reflect on God as the primary source for all creation, but in the process he also shines a light on the very nature of prayer. In considering the significance of this treatise for understanding his contribution to Franciscan prayer, Ingham identifies five themes that reflect how Scotus's work is 'exemplary of Franciscan prayer'.[6] First, Scotus understands that prayer is always dialogical; it is a two-way street, not just one-sided supplication or abstract meditation on our part. The importance of this observation rests in the centrality of relationship in the Franciscan tradition. We do not approach God as some remote or absent Creator who is uninterested in the quotidian realities of creation. Instead, God is deeply invested in creation's well-being, desiring our full flourishing and disclosing the divine self to us through creation as well as in the more formal instances of divine revelation (as contained, for instance, in sacred Scripture and most fully in Jesus Christ).

Second, Ingham notes that Scotus recognizes that 'the spiritual ascent is an affirmative journey'.[7] Prayer is not primarily about a method of *via negativa*, nor is it a journey of apophatic meditation. Rather than being interested in approaching God by means of what God *is not*, Scotus focuses on the ways in which God reveals God-self to creation in concrete, direct and kataphatic ways. It is not a matter of establishing an either/or, such as suggesting that the *via negativa* approach is not an acceptable spiritual method, but rather Scotus invites us to direct our attention to the ways in which God can be discovered in the world around us and in each other. In this way, Scotus follows his Franciscan predecessors in their preference for approaching prayer as an embodied, incarnate and empirical experience.

Third, Scotus's preference for the kataphatic or affirmative journey of prayer reflects his belief that prayer is inherently a rational experience. Nowhere does he deny the affective or visceral element of prayer, which is key to many of his Franciscan predecessors, including Bonaventure and Angela, but he is sceptical of those who assert that the spiritual journey is non-rational or even anti-intellectual. Put in modern parlance, we might think about this aspect of Scotus's approach to prayer as the marriage of *faith and reason*; they are complementary and interdependent rather than antithetical.

Fourth, like many others we have examined in this book so far, Scotus's Franciscan spirituality begins with an affirmation of the goodness of the material world and proceeds from there towards God. This element of Scotus's approach is reminiscent of Bonaventure's *Itinerarium Mentis in Deum*, where one begins the journey into God with creation, learning to see God reflected in all that has been loved into existence. For all the understandable consternation about Scotus's complex and detailed philosophical thinking, he nevertheless rejects an abstract and purely intellectual understanding of prayer. We come to discover God, and in the process find our true selves, by means of the world that God has brought into existence and of which we are also a part.

Finally, Scotus was a thinker deeply indebted to the thought of St Augustine. One of the ways Augustine's influence comes through in the approach to prayer Scotus outlines is in his insistence that we must be aided by God in our spiritual journeys. Prayer is not something that originates with us, but something that begins and is sustained by God. Throughout his own writings, Augustine talks frequently about how divine grace – the gift of God's very self to us as Holy Spirit – functions in our lives. What we come to recognize is that the desire to pray, the inauguration of the spiritual journey and the sustaining of that pilgrimage of faith are all the result of grace or divine aid.[8]

Clearly a man whose scholarly work began with prayer and centred on prayer as a way of life, Scotus offers many theological contributions that shed light on a Franciscan perspective of what it means to talk about God and what it means to talk about us. And the thread that knits both of these themes together is Scotus's maintenance of the absolute primacy of love. Given Scotus's tremendous contributions to a number of important theological issues that have drawn from his wisdom over the last eight centuries, it is clear that we cannot explore all that he offers. There are already several excellent introductions to his philosophical and theological thought.[9] In this chapter, we will narrow our focus on some of the spiritual insights and implications for prayer that arise from his life and work, which flow from the fivefold approach outlined earlier. Building on the Franciscan tradition that came before him, Scotus contributes to the way of prayer by aiding us in our discovery of God and our true selves.

Discovering who God is

We see the importance of Scotus's prioritization of love surface in his theological reflection on the reason for the incarnation. Since at least the end of the first Christian millennium, there has been what scholars call a 'majority opinion' about the reason or motive for God's becoming human. The general theory goes that the Word became flesh *because* Adam and Eve (as stand-ins for all of humanity) sinned and needed to be reconciled with God. Various theories offered by theologians and philosophers over the centuries have attempted to explain the nuances of how this reconciliation takes place through Christ, but they all generally agree on the proposal that had humanity not needed to be reconciled to God on account of our sinfulness, then God would not have become human.

By contrast, Scotus asserts God's unconditional love in Christ, stating that God would have entered into creation as one of us regardless of human sinfulness. Even if humanity had never sinned, the Word would still have become flesh (John 1.14). While not the first to propose this entirely orthodox approach to theorizing the reason for the incarnation, Scotus radically shifts the focus from us to God; from debt to gift; from sin to love. In many ways, it is the natural progression of the christocentric approaches to prayer found in all the Franciscans we have explored so far, especially as it concerns the prioritization of embodiment, the goodness of creation and the desire of God to draw near to creation witnessed in Scripture and in the ministry of Jesus. Prioritizing divine love as the sole motivating factor in God's plan for creation and Christ's role as the centre of that plan, Scotus believes that we ought to view the reason for the incarnation not in terms of a debt caused by human sin in need of repair, but by an action freely chosen by God and anchored in love.[10] Scotus summarizes this position himself:

> Neither is it likely that the highest good in the whole of creation is something that merely chanced to take place, and that only because of some lesser good. Nor is it probable that God predestined Adam to such a good before he predestined Christ. Yet all of this would follow, yes, and even something more absurd. If the predestination of Christ's soul was for the sole purpose of redeeming others, it would follow that in foreordaining Adam to glory, God would have had to foresee him as having fallen into sin before he could have predestined Christ to glory.[11]

That the incarnation was no mere accident or alternative plan, which God was forced to pursue solely to correct our errors, but part of the divine plan from all eternity motivated purely by love is a powerful corrective to much of the Christian spiritual tradition.

Sadly, many well-meaning people inadvertently create idols that they believe to be the God of Jesus Christ. They fashion such false gods in their own images and likenesses, projecting onto the Creator intentions and views that align not with what Jesus made clear about God's will throughout his earthly life, but with their own experience of and outlook on the world. Scotus's insights and approach to prayer provide an alternative understanding of who God is, focusing not on human logic or assumptions but reflecting instead the divine gratuity that we see in God's free and loving decision to enter into our experience as one of us. It does not take much imagination to consider the stark contrast in spiritual outlook between a prayer life that is built on a sin-centred view of atonement and one centred on an understanding of love motivating God's action in the world. Reflecting on a God who for all eternity desires to be one with us and return all of creation back to God in glory leads us in prayer to contemplate the inherent dignity and value of humanity, in which God participated through the incarnation. As our vision of the one we address in prayer changes to align with a God who is love (1 John 4.8), our own world view could begin to shift towards one that is more optimistic and communal in nature.

There is no doubt that the incarnation played a significant role in the spirituality of Scotus. As someone attuned to recognize signs of God's love in the world, Scotus's personal prayer almost certainly involved meditation on the immense generosity and limitless care God has for God's own creation. Scotus's theological reflection on creation is linked to his understanding of the incarnation; namely, that God is not conditioned or constrained by anything outside Godself. That is why he is so insistent that sin cannot be the primary motivation for the incarnation, because that would imply that God could be cajoled or coerced into doing or not doing something, which would infringe on divine freedom. Instead, God's will is entirely uninhibited, which Scotus describes in terms of the absolute primacy of the will. For this reason, Scotus views the created world as contingent – it is not necessary, but freely loved into existence by the Creator. Like Bonaventure, who recognized God's imprint in all creatures or Angela, who beautifully proclaimed that 'the world is pregnant with God', Scotus sees in all elements of creation reflections of God's utter freedom and the divine love that is the reason that anything exists at all when God, in complete divine self-sufficiency, had no external motivation to create the cosmos. In this way, Scotus's prayer is shaped by the continual discovery of who God is: the loving, merciful, generous Creator who so loves the world that God enters into it as one of us.

Discovering who we are

If the incarnation serves as the most explicit and concrete sign of God's love, while also glorifying humanity through God's physical entry into our world, then the creation of humanity must reflect the love of God in tremendous ways and to unfathomable degrees. Put simply, Scotus believed that God loved each individual aspect of creation – human and non-human alike – into existence and celebrates the particular character of that creature before anything shared in common with others. The technical philosophical term developed to express this is *haecceitas* (literally 'this-ness' in Latin). If we look closely at the meaning of *haecceitas*, we see the inherent dignity that is ascribed to humanity – and later to all of creation – which arises from the principle that individuation (that which makes each unique creature what it is) is the result of God's direct creative work. In some of his early lectures as a theology instructor at Oxford, Scotus rejects a number of previously held theories about the nature of individuation.[12] Scotus found these proposals inadequate.[13] It seemed to him that these views were beneath the obvious dignity of God's free and loving creative work. One thing these other proposals often held in common was the idea that God created the 'what' (*quidditas* in Latin) of something first – such as 'horse-ness' or 'human-ness' – and only secondarily modified that generic substance into a particular individual entity. Instead, Scotus insisted, individuation is rooted in the very substance of a thing or person and not simply its accidental attributes (shape, colour, number, and so on), as adherents to Aristotle's view held.[14]

Allan Wolter explains the significance of Scotus's development of the notion of haecceity:

> [Scotus] makes an important claim, that where rational beings are concerned it is the person rather than the nature that God primarily desired to create. His remark is in answer to an objection that individuals do not pertain to the order of the universe, for order is based on priority and posteriority, and individuals are all on par with one another. Not only do individuals pertain to the order of God's universe, Scotus retorts, but, in communicating 'his goodness as something befitting his beauty, in each species' he delights in producing a multiplicity of individuals. 'And in those beings which are

the highest and most important, it is the individual that is primarily intended by God' (*Ordinatio* II, d. 3, n. 251).[15]

This principle has dramatic implications for our lived experience of community, society and faith. Scotus argues for the primacy of God's creative intention in the creation of every single person. Therefore, we cannot limit the reading of Genesis 1.31 to suggest that humanity in general was created 'very good', but that each and every person was created very good. Wolter goes on to explain that this notion of haecceity, when applied to the human person, 'would seem to invest each with a unique value as one singularly wanted and loved by God, quite apart from any trait that person shares with others or any contribution he or she might make to society'.[16] In other words, it is not what we do, what we have or how we act that makes us loved by God and worthy of love from others. Rather, it is *who we are* – individually created, willed and loved into being by God – that is the source of our dignity and value.

Though it is not always easy to see given its presentation within technical and nuanced philosophical arguments, Scotus's spirituality and understanding of prayer follows from and contributes to what began with Francis and Clare of Assisi. The centrality of the incarnation is the first notable point of continuity, which reminds us of the deeply relational perspective of the Franciscan view of God. Grounding one's activity, that of scholarship or praxis, with an awareness of the inherent dignity and value of all individuals and creation further reflects Francis's own attitudinal conversion and disposition towards solidarity in prayer. The Scotist notion of *haecceitas* gives the relational sense of Franciscan 'lived prayer' a theological and philosophical anchor.

This is perhaps most clearly seen in the way that Scotus builds on the nascent insight about human dignity and value in Francis of Assisi's writings. There's a striking line in one of Francis's *Admonitions* in which he says: 'what a person is before God, that he is and no more.'[17] The immediate context for this short sermon is the increasing confidence and even arrogance of some of the early Franciscan friars as their ministry began to attract a large number of the faithful who appreciated their down-to-earth approach to pastoral care and accessibility in preaching. Francis was concerned that some of these friars were losing sight of their true identities – who it is they really are and why it is that they're doing the work of ministry in the first place. In response, Francis admonishes them to recall that their true selves are known fully by God and that who we are in God's eyes is *who we really are*. Scotus takes this insight as a starting point for his theory of *haecceitas*. Why is it that who we are before God is *really who we are*? Because God has individually loved each of us into existence and our identities are unrepeatable, irreplaceable and absolutely unique. The problem is, as Francis understood well, that we can quickly lose sight of our true selves, tempted to think that we are better or worse than the lovable and unique creature of God that we actually are.

It is so easy to be distracted from seeking out who we really are through discovering God, because we are confronted in our modern, digital age with a constant barrage of advertising and messaging that subtly or directly encourages us to doubt ourselves, to buy products to compensate for our apparent weaknesses, and to strive to be something better or at least someone different. As a result, we often spend much of our time and energy trying to recreate ourselves into what we want or think we ought to be or what others tell us we should be. The late American Trappist monk and author Thomas Merton, who was profoundly influenced by Scotus, popularized this spiritual distraction as pursuit of the 'false self'.[18] Rather than seeking to conform ourselves to some false self, we should turn towards God to discover our true selves because God is the author of the beautiful work of art that is each of us. Scotus teaches us that prayer is as much about coming to know ourselves better as it is about coming to know God. And for those for whom fear, self-consciousness or a sense of inadequacy prevents them from praying, Scotus boldly proclaims that we are already good enough and worthy of God's love because our very existence is the greatest sign of God's incomprehensible affection for each and every one of us regardless of who we are, how we are perceived by others or what we may have done.

Scotus has much to teach us today about living in a grace-filled world. Retrieval of Scotus's spiritual insights that helped shape the Franciscan way of prayer can help guide us in our contemporary world. While some will insist that the fear, greed and violence of today has replaced the goodness in our world, Scotus's work is founded on and supported by faith and hope that transcends the challenges of the present time to recall the absolute source of our being – God's love. As we pause to reflect and pray, may we look to Scotus's prayerful philosophical insights to find God's presence in our world so that we may work for the well-being of all our brothers and sisters, each of whom God has also individually loved into existence. Such prayer should lead us from our place of contemplation and reflection back into the world with responses of loving action.

Questions for reflection or discussion

1 Love is the central theme in Scotus's spiritual outlook. It shapes his understanding of God and God's action, as well as creation and our place within it. How does love factor into your spiritual journey and prayer life?

2 Scotus rejects sin as the reason God became human. What do you think about this? How might a renewed sense of God's motivation for the incarnation affect your spirituality and prayer journey?

3 Our contemporary world can be a very distracting place and the messages that confront us can be discouraging, challenging our sense of dignity, value and worth. Yet Scotus's emphasis on *haecceitas* as the principle at the core of our identity proclaims we are not only worthy of dignity and value but also individually loved into existence and known by God. In what ways does this insight inspire and challenge your sense of self? How might it affect the way you pray?

6

The way of the Franciscans continues

In his magisterial multi-volume study of the history of Christian mysticism, Bernard McGinn describes the arrival of the Franciscan spiritual tradition in the early thirteenth century as 'the New Mysticism'.[1] He recounts the novelty of 'apostolic renewal', meaning that Francis, Clare and their followers were not content merely to 'flee the world' (*fuga mundi*) as many religious communities had understood their commitment to Christian discipleship. Instead, there was an unmitigated embrace of the goodness of the world, which required a going forth, a surrender of possessions in order to embrace radical itinerancy and a prioritization of relationship, especially with the most marginalized and vulnerable in society. The model of Christian discipleship characteristic of the Franciscan tradition was not simply to imitate the first followers of Christ but to 'follow the teaching and footprints' of Jesus Christ himself.[2] The fecundity and depth of this seemingly simple insight generated the diverse spiritual tradition we have explored throughout this book. But the richness of that inspiration, the timeliness and relevance of the 'New Mysticism' of the Franciscan tradition, did not end in the thirteenth century. It continued to blossom for centuries, inspiring generations of women and men to deepen their relationship with God and ground themselves in the teachings of the gospel.

This chapter, the last stop on our prayer journey through Lent, offers a brief survey of just some of the many sources of spirituality that have contributed to the way of the Franciscans in the generations that followed the first Franciscans who have accompanied us on our prayerful pilgrimage so far. The samplings that follow are just that: a taste of the continuing diversity of Franciscan prayer as attested to by the lives and through the writings of these women and men who were inspired to follow Christ more authentically after the example of Francis and Clare of Assisi.

Jacopone da Todi (c. 1230–1306)

The Franciscan friar Jacopone da Todi is one of the best-known medieval friars you didn't realize you already knew. A poet of rare skill, he has long been attributed with composing the famous hymn known in Latin as the *Stabat Mater*, a title that comes from the opening lines *Stabat Mater dolorosa*, or 'sorrowful Mother standing', in reference to Mary the mother of Jesus who is depicted standing at the cross of her son. Translated hundreds of times over the centuries, it has inspired dozens of the world's greatest composers to set it to music, which is then often sung or performed during the season of Lent, especially on Good Friday. This particular hymn opens with the familiar lines, here translated into English from the original Latin:

> At the Cross her station keeping,
> Stood the mournful Mother weeping,
> Close to Jesus to the last.
> Through her heart, his sorrow sharing,
> All his bitter anguish bearing,
> Now at length the sword had passed.
>
> Oh, how sad and sore distress'd
> Was that Mother highly blest
> Of the sole-begotten One!
> Christ above in torment hangs;
> She beneath beholds the pangs
> Of her dying glorious Son.[3]

While most scholars affirm the likelihood of Jacopone's authorship, it remains a disputed question given the lack of absolutely verifiable corroboration and occasional attributions – though likely spurious – to other medieval authors.

Regardless of whether Jacopone was the originator of the *Stabat Mater*, we do know for certain that he is the author of dozens of poems and canticles collected in a series dubbed *The Lauds*.[4] Born sometime between 1230 and 1236, less than a decade after Francis of Assisi's death, Jacopone came from a wealthy aristocratic family. He initially studied law and finance and practised these trades for several years. He also married Vanna di Bernardino di Guidone around the year 1266. What happened between then and his recorded entrance into the Order of Friars Minor around 1278 is not known, though it is reasonable to assume he became a widower during that time.

Upon entering the Franciscan Order, he was captivated by zeal for the originating vision of Francis and Clare, especially as it related to evangelical poverty and a life of penance. This is seen in the numerous disputes he engaged in, which were motivated in large part by the emergence of the 'spiritual movement' of the late thirteenth century among a group of Franciscans who felt the order had begun moving away from Francis's founding vision. This zeal appears throughout his poetry, sometimes coming across in caustic or dismissive lines about those friars he felt had abandoned the 'true' Franciscan spirit. At other times, we see in his poetry a prayerful reflection on the virtues of Franciscan spirituality, again emphasizing the importance of penance and poverty, though without the vitriol directed at his perceived enemies. Such is the case in *Laud 4*, entitled 'On Penitence', a fitting poem for meditation during the season of Lent.

> Lofty penitence, suffering endured for love's sake,
> You are precious indeed, for through you heaven
>   is won.
> Not imposed from without, but embraced by my
>   will,
> I forge you into joy. To the well-ordered soul
> The only real suffering is sin;
> All other pain is joy in potency.

The damned know nothing of this –
Fleeing suffering, they find joy in sin.
O admirable self-hatred, master of all suffering,
You do not take offense, so you do not need to
　　pardon;
Loving all men, you recognize one enemy only
Worthy of hatred: the sin in yourself.

Self-love, at the opposite pole – you hold no man
　　dear.
Quick to take umbrage, slow to forgive,
Your enemies are legion; in you hell has already
　　begun.
O lofty Penitence, rooted in self-hatred, free gift of
　　love,
Put to rout, I pray you, Self-love and all his co-
　　horts,
Who darken the light of the soul.

Penitence is threefold: Contrition first wins for-
　　giveness;
Confession then makes the soul once more pleas-
　　ing to God;
And satisfaction cancels the debt due.
Similarly, sin inflicts three types of wounds;
It offends God, destroys our likeness to Him,
And delivers us into the hands of the Evil One.[5]

It doesn't take much effort to see how Jacopone draws from and builds upon the Franciscan spirituality he inherits: emphasis on the virtue of penance, the inclination to personify virtues and vices, and the necessity of such penitence in order to live a spiritually robust life in grace.

Like Clare, Bonaventure and Angela, Jacopone also has a sense of a pattern of prayer or path of contemplation. It varies throughout his poetry, but one explicit instance in which he proposes his own

form of an *Itinerarium,* or journey of the soul, appears in *Laud 45,*
entitled 'The Five Ways in Which God Reveals Himself.' The full
text reads:

The Lord appears to me in this life in five ways:
He who ascends to the fifth has scaled a great
     height.

The first is the state of fear, the second healing love;
The third manifestation is of tender sustenance,
Followed in turn by fatherly love
and lastly by conjugal love, the love of the bride-
     groom.

In the first stage the Lord God in His power
Raises my soul from the dead;
Putting to flight the demons who bound me in
     error,
He touches the heart with contrition.

The reawakened and still fragile soul
Is then visited by the Healer,
Who nurses and comforts
And strengthens with Sacraments.

My Love then appears as the noble companion
Who succors me and saves me from my wretched-
     ness;
He endows me with virtues that lead to salvation.
Can I leave hidden, unsung, the good He has
     wrought?

In the fourth mode He appears as a tender father
With gifts of great largesse;
Once the soul tastes of that goodness, that love,
It exults in its inheritance.

In the fifth mode Love leads me to the conjugal bed
And I lie in the embrace of the Son of God. O my
    soul,
Led by grace, you are the queen of the angels,
In wondrous fusion transformed into Christ.[6]

As is more frequently the case throughout the Franciscan spiritual tradition than is popularly recognized, the use of feminine imagery by male authors – such as we see in Jacopone's description of the 'fifth mode' of 'conjugal love' in *Laud 45* – is itself a distinctive form of poetic and prayerful reflection.[7]

One additional theme in Jacopone's spiritual poetry that resonates with other early Franciscan figures is his use of mirror imagery. As with everyone we have examined so far in this book, this is another example of diversity within the tradition – there is continuity in theme, but distinctive elements in each contribution. Perhaps the clearest illustration of this is found in his lengthy *Laud 39*, entitled 'How the Life of Jesus is the Mirror of the Soul'. Some key selections include:

To see my deformities in the mirror of truth,
The life of Jesus Christ,

To see them, Lord,
In that blinding light!

Once I looked on myself as a person of some im-
    portance
And my self-esteem helped to brighten my days.

But as I peered into that mirror the reflected light
Lit up my life, in mired depths.

Looking into that mirror and then
At the vile-smelling pit into which I had sunk,

I wept bitterly
At the chasm between the two.

I saw my faith – it was diffidence;
My hope was presumption, full of vanity;

I saw my charity –
Love half-spoiled;

One look and my world dissolved
In dizzying, turbulent confusion.

In that mirror I saw my notion of justice –
A denial of true virtue, robbing God of His honor,

Condemning the innocent
And sparing the evildoer.

Oh, the iniquity of it all! To love myself, the male-
    factor,
And deny love to Him to whom it is due![8]

It is always important to contextualize these medieval reflections, noting that 'love of self' in this context is really shorthand for selfishness, pride and arrogance rather than healthy self-esteem or self-care. Jacopone uses the mirror, which can be an instrument of disordered self-love in the case of vanity, to highlight rightly ordered love inspired by love of God. In many ways, we might see in Jacopone's use of mirror imagery a sort of hybrid between Clare and Bonaventure. Like Clare, the mirror serves as a kind of examination of conscience, which challenges the viewer to consider more deeply how they ought to imitate Christ in the world. And like Bonaventure, Jacopone sees the whole of Christ's life as the object of meditation as opposed to simply the cross, as important as it clearly is for him too.

For as much as Jacopone's poetry is remembered for the scathing social and ecclesial criticism it often contained, it is also profoundly prayerful and offers an important contribution to the way of the Franciscans. His *Lauds* take some of the central themes of the tradition and, through the process of composing original verse, invite readers to slow down and meditate on the spiritual truths he sought to express.

Catherine of Bologna (1413–1463)

The fifteenth century was a time of significant renewal for communities of women religious in the Franciscan tradition. The most notable instance is seen in the major reforms of the Second Order of St Clare by Colette of Corbie (1381–1447), who founded a monastery around 1410 and sought to return to a vision of primitive Franciscan life as she understood it. Certain Poor Clare monasteries that follow Colette's reforms continue to exist today and are known as the Colettines.[9] While not a member of the newly founded reform movement established by Colette, Catherine of Bologna – as she came to be known, having been born in that city – offers some interesting perspectives on Franciscan prayer in her distinctive writings.

Catherine was born in 1413 to a wealthy family that sent her to study in the court of the influential Este Family, who ruled as princes of the Holy Roman Empire over parts of the Lombardy region of today's Italy. Coincidentally, some of the Franciscan reform movements, like that of Colette, had taken hold in the region. The Franciscan way of life attracted Catherine who, in 1431 in the city of Ferrara, entered a Franciscan community of women who had adopted the Rule of St Clare. Something of a renaissance woman, Catherine was not only well educated but she was also an artist and musician. Just a few years after her entrance into the Ferrara community, a dispute broke out that led to her and about a dozen other sisters leaving for a new monastery in Bologna. Shortly thereafter, Catherine was elected abbess of the community.

Catherine's primary spiritual text is titled *The Seven Spiritual Weapons*, which 'combines elements of the monastic tradition of spiritual combat with the Franciscan concentration on the imitation of Christ'.[10] In a creative mystical turn, Catherine focuses on what she considers to be God's 'hiddenness' in Christ's passion and death. Whereas much of the Franciscan tradition focuses on the revelatory nature of the incarnation and Christ's whole paschal mystery, Catherine is something of an outlier in her more apophatic approach to God's self-disclosure in history. Her understanding of the hiddenness of God and the struggles facing believers with sin and temptation led her to emphasize the need for 'spiritual weapons' to overcome such challenges. These 'weapons', which are more accurately ascetical spiritual practices, are intended to train believers to place all their trust in God and continually turn to God for strength, support and love. The seven spiritual weapons are:

1 Diligence or solicitude in doing good.
2 Mistrust of self.
3 Trust in God.
4 Memory of the pilgrimage of Christ (his life, death and resurrection).
5 *Memento mori* (the practice of meditating on one's own eventual death).
6 Memory of the good works of paradise.
7 Memory of Holy Scripture.[11]

Like Jacopone and others before her, Catherine's focus on the self is less about the modern notion of self-care and esteem and more about distrust of one's own selfish inclinations or arrogance, which continues to challenge many people even today. In keeping with the Franciscan tradition of mediation on the cross of Christ, Catherine centers her spiritual reflections on Christ's Passion, encouraging contemplation on this salvific act of God as the greatest sign of divine love.

We see this most clearly in her fourth spiritual weapon when she invites the reader to meditate on the humanity of Christ and the actions recounted in the Gospels. She writes that, in prayer, we ought to keep 'always before the eyes of our minds the presence of his most chaste and virginal humanity', and that 'every other [spiritual] weapon will achieve little without this one which surpasses all the rest'.[12] After exhorting her readers to meditate continually on the life of Christ, Catherine offers a prayer of praise for Christ's Passion, which seems especially fitting given our prayer journey through Lent:

> O most glorious passion and cure for all our wounds. O mother most faithful, who lead your children to the heavenly Father. O true and gentle refuge in all adversities. O supportive nurse who guide child-like minds to the heights of perfection. O refulgent mirror, who illuminate those who look at you and recognize their deformities. O impenetrable shield who most smartly defend those who hide behind you. O manna suffused with every fulsome sweetness, you are the one who guards those who love you from every deadly poison. O ladder most high who raise up to infinite goods those who fly upward upon you. O true and restorative hospice for pilgrim souls. O ever flowing font who provide drink for the thirsty who are inflamed for you. O abundant sea for those who row on you in their derelict boat. O sweet olive tree who stretch your branches through all the universe. O spouse, gentle to the soul which is always in love with you and does not look toward others.[13]

Catherine's reflections are poetic and creative, offering stunning and evocative imagery upon which to meditate on the Passion of Christ. Her originality notwithstanding, many of the key themes we have seen regularly appearing in the writings of her Franciscan predecessors are present throughout her writing. For example, we hear echoes of Bonaventure's use of imagination in prayer and Angela's embodied mysticism, the mirror imagery of Clare and Bonaventure, the incarnational focus of Francis and Scotus, and the centrality of the cross common across all Franciscan approaches to prayer.

Catherine's sixth weapon is profoundly Franciscan in its invitation to meditate on the goodness of God's heavenly reward for those who do God's will. Her distinctive approach to attaining this is conditioned by the need that all sinners have to recall the divine source of all creation and to embrace ascetical practices in order to remind us that all goodness comes from and should return to God. She even references Francis by name and cites one of his admonitions to bolster her claim that all goodness comes from God and that we ought not even to pretend the good works we perform or the good things we enjoy are of our own making. She closes the section on the sixth weapon with the following meditation:

> So, beloved sisters, be strong and constant in persevering in doing good solely for the pure love of our Lord God and hope firmly in the goods of paradise so that you can finally reach them saying together with our seraphic St. Francis: 'Those who are just await me until you reward me' (Ps 142:8).'[14]

Finally, with zealousness reminiscent of Bonaventure, Catherine spends the greatest amount of time in *The Seven Spiritual Weapons* reflecting on the seventh, which is about meditating on holy Scripture. In her opening reflection on Scripture, she reiterates her intention to provide a guide or programme for others – especially other Franciscan sisters – who are interested in drawing closer to God and avoiding sin and temptation. The most important way one does this, Catherine argues in line with Franciscan predecessors like Bonaventure, is by continually calling to mind sacred Scripture. She writes that, with regard to the Bible, 'we must carry [the Scripture] in our hearts and from which, as from a most devoted mother, we must take counsel in all things we have to do'. She adds:

> Therefore, dearest sisters, let not the daily readings that you read in choir and at table go without effect; and let the thoughts which you hear each day in the gospels and epistles at Mass be new letters sent to you by your heavenly spouse.[15]

Inspired by the vision of Christian discipleship modelled by Francis and Clare of Assisi, and developed in diverse and creative ways by generations of Franciscans before her, Catherine offers her own engaging and instructive contribution to this inclusive tradition of prayer. With her emphasis on the Passion and cross of Christ, her seven instructions provide us with much to consider during our prayer journey through Lent.

Solanus Casey (1870–1957)

The last Franciscan we will consider is a more contemporary contributor to the Franciscan way of prayer. I have selected Blessed Solanus Casey to close our exploration of Franciscan approaches to prayer, not because he is the last contributor in this diverse centuries-old tradition but because, in many ways, his life and spirituality reflect the founding vision of Francis as the medieval saint lived it himself. Born on 25 November 1870 in the United States to parents who emigrated from Ireland, Solanus Casey spent the early years of his life working on the family farm. He was baptized Bernard Francis Casey, named after his father, and was given the religious name Francis Solanus when he entered the Franciscan Capuchin Order in 1897. Like St Francis, Solanus was someone who entered religious life after having spent a considerable amount of time pursuing other paths, such as finding the right trade. Whereas Francis worked occasionally in his father's clothing business and for a time wanted to be a knight, Solanus travelled around the American Midwest seeking meaningful employment. Discernment led him to consider a life of ministry in general and, after a short-lived attempt at the local diocesan seminary, he eventually found his way to the Franciscans.

Solanus was not a naturally gifted student, which is why the diocesan formation programme did not work out for him. Unfortunately, the diocesan clergy and seminary professors mistook Solanus's lack of academic aptitude for a sign of a general intellectual or practical ineptitude and therefore discriminated against him. Fortunately, the Capuchin Franciscans recognized God's call in his life and welcomed him into religious life. While the Capuchin archives in the Midwestern United States contain several volumes of Solanus's writings, many of which are correspondence and other practical texts, he never wrote a learned treatise or developed a formal spiritual text as we have seen in many other instances throughout this book. In this way, his own written legacy resembles Francis and Clare, who were occasional writers with limited education and demonstrated their spirituality primarily through a life of prayer rather than in written form. The limitations of formal education and the perception – both by self and others – of intellectual inadequacy make Solanus's story similar to Francis's, even more so than Clare's. Francis is remembered to have referred to himself as an *idiota* in Latin, which means 'an uneducated person'. It was a bit of an exaggeration, but it nevertheless reflected the disparity in relation to Clare's more formal education as a low-ranking noblewoman or Bonaventure's highly advanced education as a university professor and that of the founder of the Franciscan movement.

Throughout his many decades of ministry in American cities like New York and Detroit, Solanus was 'known for his deep life of prayer, his example of simplicity and humility, and especially for his charity toward the sick and the poor, and for his attentiveness to non-Catholics'.[16] It was by his example, his preaching not necessarily in erudite essays or fancy liturgical homilies but in concrete, practical and inspiring deeds, that he came to be recognized for his sanctity and commitment to prayer. In the discrete instances of daily interactions among those he served, Solanus embodied Francis of Assisi's practice of becoming 'a living prayer', and the people around him took notice.

Among his disparate sayings collected by those advancing his cause for canonization, we find clues about how Solanus received and embodied many of the most significant insights of Franciscan prayer we have examined throughout this book. For example, Solanus focused a lot on the cross of Christ and connected it to his understanding of contemporary discipleship and the challenges of ministry. He said, 'Crosses [are] the best school wherein to learn appreciation for the love of Jesus Crucified', adding: 'If we only try to show the dear Lord good will and ask Him for resignation to the crosses He sends or permits to come our way, we may be sure sooner or later they will turn out to have been just so many blessings in disguise.'[17] Taking seriously the Franciscan commitment to model one's whole life on Christ and to 'walk in the footprints' of Jesus, Solanus acknowledged that the demands of ministry can be immense and, at times, exhausting. And yet, in such moments, he meditated on the life of Jesus Christ as the model and guide for his perseverance in Christian service:

> Sometimes of course it becomes monotonous and extremely boring, till one is nearly collapsing, but in such cases, it helps to remember that even when Jesus was about to fall the third time, He patiently consoled the women folk and children of his persecutors, making no exceptions.[18]

In addition to his continual striving to follow the example of Jesus Christ through his ministry and service to the most disenfranchised in society, he developed what we might anachronistically describe as a 'catch phrase' for which he is still remembered. Influenced by Franciscans before him, he would regularly remind himself and exhort others to 'Thank God, ahead of time!' A curious development of the traditional expression in Latin *Deo gratias* ('Thanks be to God'), his inclusion of 'ahead of time' was an affirmation of his total confidence in God's providence and grace.[19] His spirit of gratitude transcended the linear experience of witnessing one's prayerful requests come to pass, and instead focused on the importance of gratitude in prayer and action *now*, in the moment, in the midst of the struggle. We see this insight developed at length in a letter he wrote to a Miss Mildred Maneal around the year 1945. He concludes that text with the following prayerful reflection:

> Let us, therefore, not weaken. Let us hope when darkness seems to surround us. Let us thank Him at all time and under whatever circumstances. Thank Him for our creation and our existence. Thank Him for everything – for His plans in the past

that our sins and our want of appreciation and patience have so
far frustrated and that He so often found necessary to change.
Let us thank Him for all His plans for the future – for trials
and humiliations as well as for great joys and consolations; for
sickness and whatever death He may deign to plan. And with
the inspired Psalmist, let us call all the creatures of the universe
to help us praise and adore Him Who is the Divine Beginning
and the everlasting Good – the Alpha and the Omega.[20]

A living example of the spiritual vision he preached, Solanus Casey
modelled what it meant to walk in the footprints of Jesus Christ,
draw on the guidance of the cross in practical terms, and direct
our attention to the need for gratitude not only when we can easily
recognize divine gifts received but also when we struggle to see the
presence of grace in our lives. Perhaps his major contribution to
the Franciscan way of prayer is a sign that this rich spiritual tradition did not stop in the medieval or renaissance eras, but continues
to grow, develop and inspire in the modern era too.

Among the many blessings of the Franciscan tradition for the
broader Church and world is precisely the diversity of its approaches to and practices of prayer. May the examples and guidance of the
varied range of spiritual insights contained in the way of Franciscan prayer, across the centuries and by women and men of such differing times and places, inspire you throughout the season of Lent
and beyond.

Questions for reflection or discussion

1 Jacopone da Todi was first and foremost a poet. In what ways
  does poetry play a role in your prayer life? Have you ever been
  inspired to express your experience of God or the world in
  verse? Might the psalms be a resource for your prayer journey
  through Lent?
2 Catherine of Bologna understood that prayer is a means, with
  God's grace, for confronting temptation and sin, which leads
  us away from our baptismal vocation to follow Christ. While
  her framing of prayer as a 'weapon to be deployed against a

spiritual enemy' may not sit well with all modern readers, what about her insights inspires or challenges you? Catherine's focus on the importance of Scripture is deeply Franciscan; how do you incorporate Scripture into your daily life?

3 Solanus Casey is a modern Franciscan model of Christian discipleship. How can you improve putting your faith into action wherever you happen to find yourself? In what way do you need to work on gratitude in your prayer life and daily actions?

Notes

Introduction: The diversity of Franciscan prayer

1   Francis of Assisi, 'The Testament', V:1, in *Francis of Assisi: Early Documents*, ed. Regis J. Armstrong, J. A. Wayne Hellmann and William J. Short, 3 vols (New York: New City Press, 1999–2001), 1:124. These volumes are hereafter cited as *FAED* followed by volume and page number.

2   See J. A. Wayne Hellmann, 'The Testament of Brother Francis (1226)', in *The Writings of Francis of Assisi: Rules, Testament, and Admonitions*, ed. Michael W. Blastic, Jay M. Hammond and J. A. Wayne Hellmann (St Bonaventure: Franciscan Institute Publications, 2011), p. 243.

3   Regis J. Armstrong and Ingrid J. Peterson, *The Franciscan Tradition* (Collegeville: Liturgical Press, 2010), p. xvii.

4   Francis of Assisi, 'The Later Rule', ch. I, v. 1 in *FAED* 1:100.

5   Francis of Assisi, 'The Testament', v. 14 in *FAED* 1:125.

6   William J. Short, *Poverty and Joy: The Franciscan Tradition* (Maryknoll: Orbis Books, 1999), p. 21.

7   Francis of Assisi, 'The Earlier Rule', ch. VII, v. 3 in *FAED* 1:68.

8   Francis of Assisi, 'The Later Rule', ch. V, v. 3 in *FAED* 1:102.

9   Regis J. Armstrong, 'Introduction: The Form of Life of Saint Clare', in *Clare of Assisi: Early Documents*, ed. Regis J. Armstrong (New York: New City Press, 2006), p. 106. This volume is hereafter cited as *CAED* followed by page number.

10 Timothy J. Johnson, 'Introduction', in *Franciscans at Prayer*, ed. Timothy J. Johnson (Leiden: Brill, 2007), p. vii.

11 Gemma Simmonds, *The Way of Ignatius: A Prayer Journey through Lent* (London: SPCK, 2018), p. 3.

12 Thomas of Celano, 'The Remembrance of the Desire of a Soul', book II, v. 190, in *FAED* 2:369.

13 Thomas of Celano, "The Remembrance', book II, v. 214, in *FAED* 2:387.

14 André Vauchez, *Francis of Assisi: The Life and Afterlife of a Medieval Saint*, tr. Michael F. Cusato (New Haven: Yale University Press, 2012), p. 269.

15 Thomas Merton, *New Seeds of Contemplation* (New York: New Directions, 1961), p. 31. For more on his Franciscan influence, see Daniel P. Horan, *The Franciscan Heart of Thomas Merton: A New Look at the Spiritual Inspiration of His Life, Thought, and Writing* (Notre Dame: Ave Maria Press, 2014).

1 Francis of Assisi: Solitude and relationship

1 Dominic V. Monti, *Francis and His Brothers: A Popular History of the Franciscan Friars* (Cincinnati: Franciscan Media, 2009), p. 11.

2 Thomas of Celano, 'The Life of Saint Francis', ch. III, v. 6, in *FAED* 1:187.

3 Michael Cusato, 'The Renunciation of Power as a Foundational Theme in Early Franciscan History', in *The Early Franciscan Movement (1205–1239): History, Sources, and Hermeneutics* (Spoleto: Centro Italiano di Studi Sull'alto Medioevo, 2009), p. 37. Also, see Michael Cusato, *La renunciation au pouvoir chez les Frères Mineurs au 13e siècle*, unpublished PhD thesis (Université de Paris IV – Sorbonne, 1991).

4 See the opening of the *Regula bullata* in *FAED* 1:100.

5 Francis of Assisi, 'The Later Rule', ch. VI, vv. 1–6 in *FAED* 1:103, emphasis added.

6 Francis of Assisi, 'A Letter to the Entire Order', vv. 27–9 in *FAED* 1: 118, adapted by author.

7 'The Assisi Compilation', no. 14, in *FAED* 2:130.

8 Thomas of Celano, 'The Life of Saint Francis', ch. XXX, v. 84 in *FAED* 1:254.

9 Norbert Nguyên-Van-Khanh, *The Teacher of His Heart: Jesus Christ in the Thought and Writings of St. Francis* (St Bonaventure: Franciscan Institute Publications, 1994), pp. 109–10. Also, see Daniel P. Horan, 'Revisiting the Incarnation: What is (and is not) the "Franciscan Approach to Christ"', in *Francis of Assisi and the*

Future of Faith: Exploring Franciscan Spirituality and Theology in the Modern World (Phoenix: Tau Publishing, 2012), pp. 115–30.

10   Francis of Assisi, 'The Earlier Rule', ch. XXIII, v. 1 in *FAED* 1:81–2.

11   Michael W. Blastic, 'Prayer in the Writings of Francis of Assisi and the Early Brothers', in *Franciscans at Prayer*, ed. Timothy J. Johnson (Leiden: Brill, 2007), p. 3.

12   For a good, detailed commentary on this chapter and the whole *Regula bullata*, see William J. Short, 'The Rules of the Lesser Brothers', in *The Writings of Francis of Assisi: Rules, Testament, and Admonitions*, ed. Michael W. Blastic, Jay M. Hammond and J. A. Wayne Hellmann (St Bonaventure: Franciscan Institute Publications, 2011), esp. pp. 161–204.

13   Francis of Assisi, 'The Later Rule', ch. V, vv. 1–2, in *FAED* 1:102, emphasis added. This is also seen in the 'The Earlier Rule' in *FAED* 1:68–9.

14   Francis of Assisi, 'A Letter to Brother Anthony of Padua', in *FAED* 1:107.

15   Francis of Assisi, 'Later Admonition and Exhortation', vv. 19–21, in *FAED* 1:46–7.

16   Francis of Assisi, 'The Prayer before the Crucifix', in *FAED* 1:40.

17   Blastic, 'Prayer in the Writings', p. 5.

18   Blastic, 'Prayer in the Writings', p. 9.

19   See André Cirino and Josef Raischl, eds., *Franciscan Solitude* (St Bonaventure: Franciscan Institute Publications, 1995).

20   Francis of Assisi, 'Religious Life in Hermitages', in *Saint Francis of Assisi, Omnibus of Sources,* ed. Marion A. Habig, 2 vols. (Cincinnati: Franciscan Media, 2008), 1:72–3, adapted.

21   See Jacques Dalarun, *Francis of Assisi and the Feminine* (St Bonaventure: Franciscan Institute Publications, 2006), esp. pp. 56–8.

22   See Grado G. Merlo, 'Eremitismo nel francescanesimo medievale', in *Eremitismo nel Francescanesimo Medievale* (Perugia: Universitá degli Sudi di Perugia, 1991), pp. 27–50.

23   Francis of Assisi, 'Letter to the Entire Order' vv. 34–7 in *FAED* 1:119.

24   See Daniel P. Horan, *Dating God: Live and Love in the Way of St. Francis* (Cincinnati: Franciscan Media, 2012), pp. 82–3.

25 Bonaventure, *The Major Legend of Saint Francis*, ch. 11, v. 1, in *FAED* 2:612.

26 This was recently published in a form more accessible to a general audience for prayer and study. See Francis of Assisi, *The Geste of the Great King: Office of the Passion of Francis of Assisi*, ed. Laurent Gallant and André Cirino (St Bonaventure: Franciscan Institute Publications, 2001).

27 For example, see Augustine, 'The Literal Meaning of Genesis', 5.16.34, in *On Genesis,* tr. Edmund Hill (New York: New City Press, 2002), p. 293; and Augustine, *Confessions*, 3.6.11, tr. Henry Chadwick (New York: Oxford University Press, 1991), p. 43.

28 See Thomas of Celano, 'The Remembrance of the Desire of a Soul', book II, ch. LXI, v. 95 in *FAED* 2:310. Also, see Thomas of Celano, 'The Life of Saint Francis', book II, ch. IV, v. 97 in *FAED* 1:266.

29 Blastic, 'Prayer in the writings', p. 13.

2 Clare of Assisi: Poverty, contemplation and the cross

1 There have been several important studies about Clare and the early Poor Clare Sisters published in recent years. For example, see Margaret Carney, *The First Franciscan Women: Clare of Assisi and Her Form of Life* (Quincy: Franciscan Press, 1993); Maria Pia Alberzoni, *Clare of Assisi and the Poor Sisters in the Thirteenth Century* (St Bonaventure: Franciscan Institute Publications, 2004); Joan Mueller, *The Privilege of Poverty: Clare of Assisi, Agnes of Prague, and the Struggle for the Franciscan Rule for Women* (University Park: Penn State Press, 2006); Lezlie S. Knox, *Creating Clare of Assisi: Female Franciscan Identities in Later Medieval Italy* (Leiden: Brill Publishers, 2008); Sr Frances Teresa OSC, *This Living Mirror: Reflections on Clare of Assisi* (London: Darton, Longman and Todd, 1995); Marco Bartoli, *Saint Clare: Beyond the Legend*, tr. Frances Teresa Downing (Cincinnati: Franciscan Media, 2010); among others.

2 William J. Short, *Poverty and Joy: The Franciscan Tradition* (Maryknoll: Orbis Books, 1999), p. 32.

3 Short, *Poverty and Joy*, p. 33.

4   Ilia Delio, 'Clare of Assisi and the Mysticism of Motherhood', in
    Franciscans at Prayer, ed. Timothy J. Johnson (Leiden: Brill, 2007),
    p. 40.

5   Bartoli, *Saint Clare*, p. 49.

6   Clare of Assisi, 'The First Letter to Agnes of Prague', vv. 15–21,
    in *CAED*, p. 45. Unless otherwise noted, all references to Clare's
    writings come from this edition.

7   Delio, 'Clare of Assisi and the Mysticism of Motherhood', p. 40.

8   For more on this subject, see Ingrid Peterson, 'Clare of Assisi's
    Letters to Agnes of Prague: Testaments of Fidelity', in *The Writings
    of Clare of Assisi: Letters, Form of Life, Testament, and Blessing*, ed.
    Michael W. Blastic, Jay M. Hammond and J. A. Wayne Hellmann
    (St Bonaventure: Franciscan Institute Publications, 2011), pp. 43–4.

9   Clare of Assisi, 'The Second Letter to Agnes of Prague', v. 7, in
    CAED, p. 47.

10 Clare of Assisi, 'The Second Letter to Agnes of Prague', vv. 11–14,
    in *CAED*, p. 48.

11 Timothy J. Johnson, 'Visual Imagery and Contemplation in Clare
    of Assisi's "Letters to Agnes of Prague"', *Mystics Quarterly* 19
    (December 1993), p. 163.

12 Delio, 'Clare of Assisi and the Mysticism of Motherhood', p. 46.

13 Regis J. Armstrong, 'Introduction', in *CAED*, p. 20.

14 Clare of Assisi, 'The Second Letter to Agnes of Prague', vv. 18–20,
    in *CAED*, p. 49.

15 Clare of Assisi, 'The Fourth Letter to Agnes of Prague', vv. 15–18,
    in *CAED*, p. 55.

16 Armstrong, 'Introduction', in *CAED*, p. 21.

17 Delio, 'Clare of Assisi and the Mysticism of Motherhood', p. 49.

18 Delio, 'Clare of Assisi and the Mysticism of Motherhood', p. 49.

19 Ilia Delio, *Clare of Assisi: A Heart Full of Love* (Cincinnati:
    Franciscan Media, 2007), p. 54.

20 Johnson, 'Visual Imagery', p. 166.

21 Johnson, 'Visual Imagery', p. 167.

22 Johnson, 'Visual Imagery', p. 168.

23 Peterson, 'Clare of Assisi's Letters to Agnes of Prague', p. 49.

24 Clare of Assisi, 'The Fourth Letter to Agnes of Prague', v. 33, in *CAED*, p. 57.

25 Delio, 'Clare of Assisi and the Mysticism of Motherhood', p. 50.

26 Delio, 'Clare of Assisi and the Mysticism of Motherhood', p. 50.

27 Clare of Assisi, 'The Third Letter to Agnes of Prague', vv. 8–14, in *CAED*, pp. 50–1.

28 Clare of Assisi, 'The Third Letter to Agnes of Prague', v. 12, in *CAED*, p. 51. For more on this motif in Clare's spirituality, see Regis J. Armstrong, 'Clare of Assisi: The Mirror Mystic', *The Cord* (1985), pp. 195–202.

29 Delio, 'Clare of Assisi and the Mysticism of Motherhood', p. 51.

30 Delio, *Clare of Assisi*, p. 27.

3 Bonaventure: Prophecy and everyday mysticism

1 Thanks to a somewhat recent and accessible translation of these titles, all contained in one volume, a broader audience can approach Bonaventure's texts. See Ewert Cousins, ed., *Bonaventure: The Soul's Journey into God, The Tree of Life, and The Life of St. Francis* (New York: Paulist Press, 1978).

2 See Charles Carpenter, *Theology as the Road to Holiness in St. Bonaventure* (New York: Paulist Press 1999); and Gregory LaNave, *Through Holiness to Wisdom: The Nature of Theology according to St. Bonaventure* (Rome: Instituto Storico dei Cappuccini, 2005).

3 Ignatius Brady, 'The History of Mental Prayer in the Order of Friars Minor', *Franciscan Studies* 1 (1951), p. 323.

4 Zachary Hayes, *Bonaventure: Mystical Writings* (Phoenix: Tau Publishing, 1999), p. 19.

5 Hayes, *Bonaventure: Mystical Writings*, p. 19.

6 Richard S. Martignetti, *Saint Bonaventure's Tree of Life: Theology of the Mystical Journey* (Roma: Frati Editori di Quaracchi, 2004), p. 40.

7 Ilia Delio, *Simply Bonaventure: An Introduction to His Life, Thought, and Writings* (New York: New City Press, 2001), p. 130.

8 Sally Ann McReynolds, 'Imagination', in *The New Dictionary of Catholic Spirituality*, ed. Michael Downey (Collegeville: Liturgical Press, 1993), p. 531.

9 See Gemma Simmonds, *The Way of Ignatius: A Prayer Journey through Lent* (London: SPCK, 2018).

10 See Ewert Cousins, 'Franciscan Roots of Ignatian Meditation', in *Ignatian Spirituality in a Secular Age*, ed. George P. Schner (Waterloo, Ontario: Wilfred Laurier University Press, 1984), pp. 53–63; and Franco Mormando, 'Ignatius the Franciscan: The Franciscan Roots of Ignatian Spirituality', unpublished lecture at Boston College (6 November 2019), recording available online at: <https://youtu.be/V6tOEmfYzgc>.
In his introduction to his translation of the *Tree of Life*, the former Jesuit and late medieval scholar Ewert Cousins notes that 'Bonaventure's *The Tree of Life* is in many respects a forerunner of Ignatian meditation, in both its subject matter and its techniques'. He adds, 'From one point of view, the Ignatian *Exercises* can be seen as an initiation into the contemplative vision that Bonaventure proposes'. Cousins, 'Introduction', in Cousins, ed., *Bonaventure*, p. 37.

11 The English translation is found in Cousins, ed., *Bonaventure*.

12 Bonaventure, *The Tree of Life*, prol. 2, in Cousins, ed., *Bonaventure*, p. 120.

13 Bonaventure, *The Tree of Life*, no. 4, in Cousins, ed., *Bonaventure*, p. 128.

14 Bonaventure, *The Tree of Life*, no. 4, in Cousins, ed., *Bonaventure*, p. 129.

15 The best translation from the original Latin into English is Bonaventure, *Bringing Forth Christ: Five Feasts of the Child Jesus*, tr. Eric Doyle (Oxford: SLG Press, 1984).

16 Bonaventure, *Five Feasts of the Child Jesus*, prol., tr. Doyle, p. 2.

17 Bonaventure, *The Tree of Life*, no. 21, in Cousins, ed., *Bonaventure*, pp. 144–5.

18 Bonaventure, *The Threefold Way*, in *Writings on the Spiritual Life*, ed. F. Edward Coughlin, *Works of St. Bonaventure*, vol. X (St Bonaventure: Franciscan Institute Publications, 2006), pp. 89–133.

19 Bonaventure, *The Threefold Way*, prol., in Coughlin, *Writings*, p. 90.

20 See Bonaventure, 'The Major Legend of Saint Francis', in *FAED* 2:525–683.

21 Bonaventure, 'The Major Legend of Saint Francis', ch. XI, in *FAED* 2:612.

22 See Chapter 1 (p. 28) for the full quote that begins, 'Unflagging zeal for prayer'.

23 Bonaventure, 'The Major Legend of Saint Francis', ch. XI, no. 3, in *FAED* 2:614.

24 Thomas Merton, *The Springs of Contemplation: A Retreat at the Abbey of Gethsemani*, ed. Jane Marie Richardson (New York: Farrar, Straus & Giroux, 1992), pp. 157–8.

25 There are many modern translations of the *Itinerarium*, including: Cousins, ed., *Bonaventure*; *Itinerarium Mentis in Deum*, ed. Philotheus Boehner and Zachary Hayes, *Works of St. Bonaventure*, vol. 2 (St Bonaventure: Franciscan Institute Publications, 2002); *The Journey of the Mind to God*, ed. Stephen F. Brown (Indianapolis: Hackett Publishing, 1993); and, most recently, Regis J. Armstrong, *Into God:* Itinerarium Mentis in Deum *of Saint Bonaventure – An Annotated Translation* (Washington, DC: Catholic University of America Press, 2020).

26 Armstrong, *Into God*, p. 176.

27 Bonaventure, *Itinerarium*, prol., no. 1, in Boehner and Hayes, p. 35.

28 Bonaventure, *Itinerarium*, ch. 1, no. 15 in Boehner and Hayes, p. 61.

29 Bonaventure, *Itinerarium*, ch. 2, no. 1, in Boehner and Hayes, p. 63.

30 Bonaventure, *Itinerarium*, ch. 4, no. 8, in Boehner and Hayes, p. 107.

31 Bonaventure, *Itinerarium*, ch. 7, no. 6, in Boehner and Hayes, p. 139.

4 Angela of Foligno: Love of Christ, love of the world

1 After Pope Francis canonized Angela, the Vatican News Service published a summary of her story, which included the spurious date of 4 January 1248 (records do show that she died on 4 January 1309, so there may be some accidental conflation of the dates). Historians have not been able to confirm the exact date or year of her birth, though the Catholic Church celebrates her feast day on 4 January. See 'St. Angela of Foligno, Franciscan online at: <www.vaticannews. va/en/saints/01/04/st--angela-of-foligno--franciscan.html>.

2 Paul Lachance, 'Introduction', in *Angela of Foligno: Complete Works*, ed. Paul Lachance (New York: Paulist Press, 1993),

p. 16. Hereafter this translation of Angela's work will be cited parenthetically as "Lachance" followed by page number.

3   Lachance, 'Introduction', p. 16.

4   Lachance, 'Introduction', p. 17.

5   See Bernard McGinn, *The Flowering of Mysticism: Men and Women in the New Mysticism – 1200–1350, The Presence of God*, vol. 3 (New York: Crossroad Publishing, 1998), p. 143, n. 167.

6   *Memorial* 3 (Lachance, pp. 139–40).

7   *Memorial* 3 (Lachance p. 140).

8   Historian Darleen Pryds attributed Angela's widespread renown and spiritual authority to her having lived a life very similar to other non-clerics and non-religious of the time, which allowed her spiritual guidance to be practical and relatable. See Darleen Pryds, *Women of the Streets: Early Franciscan Women and their Mendicant Vocation* (St Bonaventure: Franciscan Institute Publications, 2010), p. 35.

9   Angela of Foligno, *Instructions* II (Lachance, p. 224).

10   Angela of Foligno, *Instructions* III.2 (Lachance, p. 239).

11   Angela of Foligno, *Instructions* III.2 (Lachance, p. 234).

12   Angela of Foligno, *Instructions* III.2 (Lachance, p. 236). Emphasis added.

13   Angela of Foligno, *Instructions* II (Lachance, p. 236).

14   Angela of Foligno, *Memorial* VI (Lachance, p. 175).

15   Angela of Foligno, *Memorial* III (Lachance, p. 147).

16   Angela of Foligno, *Memorial* VI (Lachance, p. 174).

17   Angela of Foligno, *Memorial* IX (Lachance, p. 205).

18   Angela of Foligno, *Memorial* IX (Lachance, pp. 205–6).

19   See Katherine Wrisley Shelby, 'A Performative Christ and the Performing Penitent: Exploring the Possibility of a Feminine Franciscan Christology in Angela of Foligno's *Liber*', *Cult/ure: The Graduate Journal of Harvard Divinity School* (Fall 2012): online at: <https://projects.iq.harvard.edu/hdsjournal/book/performative-christ-and-performing-penitent>.

20   Wrisley Shelby, 'A Performative Christ'.

21   Lachance, 'Introduction', p. 100.

22   Lachance, 'Introduction', pp. 100–1.

23   Lachance, 'Introduction', p. 101.
24   Angela of Foligno, *Memorial* VII (Lachance, p. 183).
25   Francis of Assisi, 'Admonition V', nos. 7–8, in *FAED* 1:131.
26   Angela of Foligno, *Memorial* VII (Lachance, p. 184).
27   Angela of Foligno, *Memorial* V (Lachance, p. 163).
28   Francis of Assisi, 'The Testament', no. 3, in *FAED* 1:124.
29   Caroline Walker Bynum, 'The Female Body and Religious Practice
      in the Later Middle Ages', in *Fragments for a History of the Human
      Body: Part One*, ed. Michele Feher (New York: Zone Books, 1989),
      p. 163.
30   Angela of Foligno, *Memorial* VI (Lachance, pp. 169–70).
31   Angela of Foligno, *Instructions* II (Lachance, pp. 227–8).
32   Angela of Foligno, *Instructions* XXVIII (Lachance, p. 286).
33   Angela of Foligno, *Instructions* XXVIII (Lachance, p. 287).

5 John Duns Scotus: Discovering God and our true self

1   See Mary Beth Ingham, '*Fides Quaerens Intellectum*: John Duns
     Scotus, Philosophy and Prayer', in *Franciscans at Prayer*, ed.
     Timothy J. Johnson (Leiden: Brill, 2007), pp. 167–91.
2   See Daniel P. Horan, 'Light and Love: Robert Grosseteste and
     John Duns Scotus on the How and Why of Creation', *The Cord* 57
     (2007), pp. 252–3.
3   John Duns Scotus, *Tractatus De Primo Principio* 1.2, in *John
     Duns Scotus: A Treatise on God as First Principle*, tr. Allan Wolter
     (Chicago: Franciscan Herald Press, 1982), p. 2. Emphasis added.
4   Allan Wolter, 'Commentary on the *De Primo Principio* of Duns
     Scotus', in *John Duns Scotus: A Treatise on God as First Principle*,
     ed. Wolter, pp. 160–1.
5   Wolter makes reference to the Berlin manuscript (Codex B) and the
     proximity of the condensed form of Scotus's *De Primo Principio*,
     minus the philosophical argumentation, to Bonaventure's
     Itinerarium Mentis in Deum. The compiler(s) of the manuscript
     obviously found Scotus's prayers of great spiritual value to be
     included alongside Bonaventure's most acclaimed spiritual work.
6   Ingham, '*Fides Quaerens Intellectum*', p. 189.
7   Ingham, '*Fides Quaerens Intellectum*', p. 189.

8   Ingham, '*Fides Quaerens Intellectum*', p. 189.

9   For example, see Richard Cross, *Duns Scotus* (New York: Oxford University Press, 1999) and Mary Beth Ingham, *Scotus for Dunces: An Introduction to the Subtle Doctor* (St Bonaventure: Franciscan Institute Publications, 2003).

10   Mary Beth Ingham, 'Duns Scotus, Divine Delight and Franciscan Evangelical Life', *Franciscan Studies* 64 (2006), p. 343.

11   John Duns Scotus, *Ordinatio* III, dist. 7, q. 3, tr. Allan Wolter, 'John Duns Scotus on the Primacy and Personality of Christ', in *Franciscan Christology*, ed. Damian McElrath (St Bonaventure: Franciscan Institute Publications, 1994), pp. 148–51.

12   The English translation is found in Allan Wolter, *John Duns Scotus: Early Oxford Lecture on Individuation* (St Bonaventure, NY: Franciscan Institute Publications, 2005).

13   Kenan Osborne, 'Incarnation, Individuality and Diversity: How does Christ reveal the unique value of each person and thing?' *The Cord* 45 (1995), p. 25.

14   Osborne, 'Incarnation, Individuality and Diversity', p. 25.

15   Wolter, *John Duns Scotus: Early Oxford Lecture on Individuation*, p. xxi.

16   Wolter, *John Duns Scotus: Early Oxford Lecture on Individuation*, p. xxi.

17   Francis of Assisi, 'Admonition XIX', no. 2, in *FAED* 1:135.

18   See Thomas Merton, *New Seeds of Contemplation* (New York: New Directions, 1961).

6 The way of the Franciscans continues

1   See Bernard McGinn, *The Flowering of Mysticism: Men and Women in the New Mysticism – 1200–1350* (New York: Crossroad Publishing, 1998).

2   See Francis of Assisi, 'The Earlier Rule', ch. I, v. 1, in *FAED* 1:63–4.

3   '*Stabat Mater dolorosa*', in *Lyra Catholica*, tr. Edward Caswall (London: Burns & Oates, 1849), pp. 138–9.

4   See Jacopone da Todi, *The Lauds*, ed. Serge and Elizabeth Hughes (New York: Paulist Press, 1982). The lengthy introduction to this volume provides a great wealth of historical information, though

the best study of Jacopone's life and work in English remains George T. Peck, *The Fool of God: Jacopone da Todi* (Birmingham: University of Alabama Press, 1980).

5   Jacopone da Todi, 'Laud 4: On Penitence', in *The Lauds*, p. 75.

6   Jacopone da Todi, 'Laud 45: The Five Ways in Which God Reveals Himself', in *The Lauds*, pp. 157–8.

7   For more, see Jacques Dalarun, *Francis of Assisi and the Feminine*, tr. Paula Pierce and Mary Sutphin (St Bonaventure: Franciscan Institute Publications, 2006).

8   Jacopone da Todi, 'Laud 39: How the Life of Jesus is the Mirror of the Soul', in *The Lauds*, pp. 137–8.

9   See Bert Roest, *Order and Disorder: The Poor Clares between Foundation and Reform* (Leiden: Brill Publishing, 2013) and Mother Mary Francis, *The Testament of St. Colette* (Chicago: Franciscan Herald Press, 1987).

10   Regis J. Armstrong and Ingrid J. Peterson, *The Franciscan Tradition* (Collegeville: Liturgical Press, 2010), p. 96.

11   Armstrong and Peterson, *The Franciscan Tradition*, p. 96.

12   Catherine of Bologna, *The Seven Spiritual Weapons*, IV.1, tr. Hugh Feiss and Daniela Re (Toronto: Peregrina Publishing, 1999), p. 37.

13   Catherine of Bologna, *The Seven Spiritual Weapons*, IV.2–3, tr. Feiss and Re, pp. 39–40).

14   Catherine of Bologna, *The Seven Spiritual Weapons*, VI.9, tr. Feiss and Re, p. 41.

15   Catherine of Bologna, *The Seven Spiritual Weapons*, VII.2–3, tr. Feiss and Re, pp. 41–2.

16   Armstrong and Peterson, *The Franciscan Tradition*, pp. 58–9.

17   Catherine M. Odell, *Father Solanus Casey*, rev. edn (Huntington, IN: Our Sunday Visitor Publishing, 2017), p. 248.

18   Odell, *Father Solanus Casey*, p. 247.

19   Armstrong and Peterson, *The Franciscan Tradition*, p. 59.

20   Michael Crosby, *Solanus Casey: The Official Account of a Virtuous American Life* (New York: Crossroad Publishing, 2000), p. 47.